ORGANIZATION DEVELOPMENT:
ITS NATURE, ORIGINS, AND PROSPECTS

WARREN G. BENNIS

State University of New York at Buffalo

ADDISON-WESLEY PUBLISHING COMPANY

Reading, Massachusetts · Menlo Park, California

London · Amsterdam · Don Mills, Ontario · Sydney

This book is in the Addison-Wesley series:

ORGANIZATION DEVELOPMENT

Editors
Edgar Schein
Warren Bennis
Richard Beckhard

For my Mother,
RACHEL BENNIS LANGER

ISBN 0-201-00523-9
MNOPQRSTUV-DO-7987

FOREWORD

The purpose of this common foreword to all the volumes of the Addison-Wesley Series on Organization Development is twofold: (1) to give the reader some idea as to the origin and purpose of the series; and (2) to guide the reader through the content of the different books.

The series came to be because we felt there was a growing theory and practice of something called "organization development," but most students, colleagues, and managers knew relatively little about it. Many of us are highly active as OD consultants, but little has been written about what we do when we are with a client or what our underlying theory of consultation is. We were also acutely aware of the fact that, though there are common assumptions shared by most practitioners of OD, there are great individual variations in the strategies and tactics employed by different consultants. The field is still emerging and new methods are constantly being invented. It seemed appropriate, therefore, not to try to write a single text, but to give several of the foremost theorist-practitioners a chance to explain their own view of OD and their own style of working with client systems.

The authors of this series of six books represent a variety of points of view, but they do not exhaust the major approaches currently in use in OD. There are some obvious names missing—Argyris, Tannenbaum, Ferguson, Bradford, Davis, Burke—to name just a few. We hope in future volumes of the series to get these men and others to write about their theory and practice.

The six books of this series can be described as follows: Bennis presents a very broad survey of the history and present practice of OD. How and why did it come about, what is it, and what are some of the major unresolved issues in OD? The Beckhard volume is a systematic attempt to describe the various strategies and tactics employed in different kinds of OD efforts. Beckhard goes beyond his own approach and tries to build a general framework within which most OD programs can be located. The Beckhard and Bennis volumes together give the reader an excellent overview of the field.

The two volumes by Blake and Mouton and by Lawrence and Lorsch are somewhat more personalized statements of their particular views of how organizations function, how organizational excellence is to be judged, and how an OD effort can contribute to the achievement of such excellence. Both books are focused on total organization systems and attempt to show how intervention in organizations leads to constructive change and development.

The volumes by Walton and Schein are written at a more specific level. They highlight some of the day-to-day activities of the consultant as he works with a client system in the context of an OD program. Both deal with the process of the consultation itself. In the Walton book the focus is on the process by which the consultant uses himself to aid in the resolution of conflict. In the Schein book the idea of "process consultation" is introduced and explained in detail. The kinds of organizational processes which are described in these last two volumes lie at the heart of OD efforts, but the focus of the books is on the moment-to-moment behavior of the consultant rather than the overall design of the OD program.

The six books were written independently with only broad guidelines and minimum coordination by the editors. It was our hope and intention to get six very personal and unique statements, rather than a closely integrated set of "chapters." We feel that the amount of overlap is minimal, and that the books in fact complement each other very well in being written at different levels of generality. We hope that the reader will sense that the field of OD is converging toward common theories and practices, but that we are a long way from being able to produce a definitive "text" on the subject.

March 1969   Edgar H. Schein
                                                              Richard Beckhard
                                                              Warren G. Bennis

PREFACE

This book, a primer on organization development, is written with an eye toward the people in organizations who may be interested in learning more about this educational strategy as well as for those practitioners and students of organization development who may want a basic statement to learn from and to argue with. I have tried to set down what I know about this subject with a minimum of academic jargon and with a maximum of concrete examples drawn from my own and others' experience.

The book rests on three basic propositions: The first is an evolutionary hypothesis that every age develops an organizational form most appropriate to the genius of that age and that certain unparalleled changes are taking place which make it necessary to revitalize and rebuild our organizations. The second is that the only viable way to change organizations is to change their "culture," that is, to change the systems within which people work and live. A "culture" is a way of life, a system of beliefs and values, an accepted form of interaction and relating. Changing individuals, while terribly important, cannot yield the fundamental impact so necessary for the revitalization and renewal I have in mind—if our organizations are to survive and develop. Thirdly, a new *social* awareness is required by people in organizations along with its spiritual ancestor, *self-* awareness. Organizations are becoming collectively aware of their destiny and their path to guiding their destiny. This proposition asserts that social consciousness is more difficult to induce than personal awareness but more essential in the kind of world we are living in.

v

The book consists of six chapters. Chapter 1 tries to answer the question: What is organization development? Chapter 2 revolves around the question: *Why* organization development, that is, what conditions lead to the inevitability of organization development? Chapters 3 and 4 are "question and answer" chapters where I try to respond to some of the most often asked questions about organization development. In Chapter 3, I take up those questions most often asked by professional people, and in Chapter 4, I deal with those questions most frequently asked by people in organizations curious about starting organization development programs. The fifth chapter takes up the problem of "sensitivity training," and attempts to analyze the conditions underlying its failures and successes as an Organization Development strategy. The last chapter poses certain general questions which the field of Organization Development itself must deal with as best it can. I have also added a short bibliography for the curious reader.

Buffalo   W.G.B.
January 1969

CONTENTS

1

ORGANIZATION DEVELOPMENT: WHAT IT IS AND WHAT IT ISN'T

At some unmarked point during the last twenty years we imperceptibly moved out of the modern age and into a new, as yet nameless, era . . . . The old view of the world, the old tasks and the old center, calling themselves 'modern' and 'up-to-date' only a few years ago, just make no sense anymore. They still provide our rhetoric, whether of politics or science, at home or in foreign affairs. But the slogans and battle cries of all parties, be they political, philosophical, aesthetic, or scientific, no longer serve to unite for action—though they still can divide in heat and emotion. Our actions are still measured against the stern demands of the 'today,' the post-modern' world: and yet we have no theories, no concepts, no slogans—no real knowledge—about the new reality.[1]

Peter Drucker

Writing in August 1968, I find it impossible to dispute Peter Drucker's gloomy statement. The two recent national political conventions with the "new politics" have revealed the trouble we are in, and we are in trouble because we have no "real knowledge" about the new reality, this post-industrial world.

Change is the biggest story in the world today, and we are not coping with it adequately: change in the size of and movement of people; change in the nature, location, and availability of jobs; changing relations between whites and blacks, between students and professors, between workers and

---

1 The Practice of Management, P. F. Drucker. New York: Harper & Row (1954).

employers, between generations, and violent change at that; violent change in the cities; change in relations between village and town, town and city, city and nation, and, of course, change in the relations between the empires that are falling and the empires that are rising.

Human organizations are as susceptible, perhaps more so, as other social institutions are to changing times, and their rise and fall, success and failure, all testify to their vulnerability. As John W. Gardner (1965) suggests,

What may be most in need of innovation is the corporation itself. Perhaps what every corporation (and every other organization) needs is a department of continuous renewal that could view the whole organization as a system in need of continuing innovation.

Organization development (OD) is a response to change, a complex educational strategy intended to change the beliefs, attitudes, values, and structure of organizations so that they can better adapt to new technologies, markets, and challenges, and the dizzying rate of change itself. Organization development is new and still emerging, only a decade old, so its shape and potentiality are far from granted and its problems far from solved. Yet it holds promise for developing the "real knowledge" about our post-modern world.

It might be helpful at the outset to review some examples of organization development and from these illustrations develop a fuller understanding of the subject, rather than starting from an abstract, and perhaps useless, definition.

Example 1. Team Development.   Douglas McGregor (1967) was a consultant to a management group at Union Carbide in 1964. One of the explicit tasks of the consultant was to help build an "effective management team." This was defined in terms of a number of features, including: 1) understanding, mutual agreement, and identification regarding the goals of the group, 2) open communication, 3) mutual trust, 4) mutual support, 5) effective management of conflict, 6) developing a selective and appropriate use of the team concept, 7) utilizing appropriate member skills, and 8) developing appropriate leadership. I suppose that these criteria would be shared by most organizations requiring collaborative efforts.

McGregor, along with the formal head of the management group, John Paul Jones, devised a crude scale which represented as closely as possible these features of an effective team (Table 1-1):

TABLE 1-1   Team Development Scale

1. Degree of mutual trust:
   High suspicion_____High trust
   　　　(1)　　　　　　　　(4)　　　　　　　　(7)

2. Communications:
   Guarded, cautious_____Open, authentic
   　　　(1)　　　　　　　　(4)　　　　　　　　(7)

3. Degree of mutual support:
   Every man for himself_____Genuine concern
   　　　　　　　　　　　　　　　　　　for each other
   　　　(1)　　　　　　　　(4)　　　　　　　　(7)

4. Team objectives:
   Not understood_____Clearly understood
   　　　(1)　　　　　　　　(4)　　　　　　　　(7)

5. Handling conflicts within team:
   Through denial, avoidance,　　　　　　Acceptance and
   suppression, or compromise_____"working through"
   　　　　　　　　　　　　　　　　　　of conflicts
   　　　(1)　　　　　　　　(4)　　　　　　　　(7)

6. Utilization of member resources:
   Competencies　　　　　　　　　　　　Competencies
   used by team_____not used
   　　　(1)　　　　　　　　(4)　　　　　　　　(7)

7. Control methods:
   Control is imposed_____Control from within
   　　　(1)　　　　　　　　(4)　　　　　　　　(7)

8. Organizational environment:
   Restrictive, pressure　　　　　　　　Free, supportive, re-
   for conformity_____spect for differences
   　　　(1)　　　　　　　　(4)　　　　　　　　(7)

McGregor (1967, p. 172) writes:

I have seen groups make effective use of a simple rating scale (like the exhibit above) for purposes of analysis. After a little discussion of the meaning of each variable, each member fills out the form anonymously, rating his personal view of the current state of the group. The ratings are then pooled and a chart prepared by a couple of members showing the mean of the ratings and the high and low 'score' for each variable. On the basis of these data, the group discusses what aspects of its group operation need work.[2]

The main purpose of this exercise, according to McGregor, is to provide each member of the group with feedback about how others perceive the group in relation to himself and feedback about how group effectiveness can be improved.

Example 2. Intergroup Conflict. Among the recent problems facing the U.S. Department of State was unproductive divisiveness between the Foreign Service officers, sometimes referred to as "the club" or "the guild" and the administrative staff of State. The stereotyping and mutual distrust, if not downright hostility, blocked communication and reduced effectiveness enormously, for each "side" perceived the other as more threatening than any realistic overseas enemy.

During a State Department conference held at M.I.T. in early June of 1966, Chris Argyris (1967) and I divided a group of top echelon administrative officers and Foreign Service officers into two groups along functional lines. The two groups were assigned to separate rooms, and were asked to discuss three questions and to develop a list of words or phrases that would summarize their answers:

1. What qualities best describe our group?

2. What qualities best describe the other group?

3. What qualities do we predict the other group would assign to us?

As Argyris (1967, pp. 20-21) wrote:

The faculty reported that the groups became involved in the exercise and produced products that reflected validly the discussions that were held in their separate meeting rooms.

The results were as follows:

- *The Foreign Service officers saw themselves as:*
  1. Reflective
  2. Qualitative

---

2   From The Professional Manager by Douglas McGregor. Copyright 1967, McGraw-Hill Book Co., New York. Used with permission of McGraw-Hill Book Co.

3. Humanistic, subjective
4. Cultural, broad interests
5. Generalizers
6. Intercultural sensitivity
7. Detached from personal conflicts

• *The Foreign Service officers saw the administrative officers as:*

1. Doers and implementers
2. Quantitative
3. Decisive and forceful
4. Noncultural
5. Limited goals
6. Jealous of us
7. Interested in form more than substance
8. Wave of the future! (exclamation mark theirs)
9. Drones but necessary evils

• *The Foreign Service officers predicted that the administrative officers would see them as:*

1. Arrogant, snobs
2. Intellectuals
3. Cliquish
4. Resistant to change
5. Inefficient, dysfunctional
6. Vacillating and compromising
7. Effete

• *The administrative officers saw themselves as:*

1. Decisive, guts
2. Resourceful, adaptive
3. Pragmatic
4. Service-oriented
5. Able to get along
6. Receptive to change
7. Dedicated to job
8. Misunderstood
9. Useful
10. Modest! (added by the individual doing the presenting)

• *The administrative officers saw the Foreign Service officers as:*

1. Masked, isolated
2. Resourceful, serious
3. Respected
4. Inclined to stability
5. Dedicated to job
6. Necessary
7. Externally oriented
8. Cautious
9. Rational
10. Surrounded by mystique
11. Manipulative
12. Defensive

• *The administrative officers predicted that the Foreign Service officers would see them as:*

1. Necessary evil
2. Defensive, inflexible
3. Preoccupied with minutiae
4. Negative and bureaucratic
5. Limited perspective
6. Less cultural (educated clerks)
7. Misunderstood
8. Practical
9. Protected
10. Resourceful

After the lists were produced, the two groups assembled together and then proceeded to discuss their lists and to be questioned by the other group with respect to their perceptions. The discussion was intense, high-pitched, noisy, argumentative, good-humored, and finally, several hours later, thoughtful. It appeared as if each side moved to a position where they at least understood the other side's point of view.

Example 3. Confrontation Meeting. The Director of a small and spectacularly successful educational R&D firm called to see whether I could help their rapidly growing nonprofit enterprise. He felt that the organization had grown too rapidly; that the project teams were not in communication, and worse, were extremely competitive; that the organization had to make some serious decisions regarding its future, especially with respect to whether or not it would produce and market the wonderfully creative things it was inventing for school systems; and besides all this, he felt woefully behind in his own creative work and wondered whether or not his office could be managed more effectively. He also made it clear to me that the people wanted nothing to do with T-groups or sensitivity training. I spent a morning with the Director and his entire professional staff, consisting of some 40 individuals, almost all of them holding PhD's and joint appointments at nearby universities.

Everything that the Director had related to me was confirmed by interviews with the professional staff, except that they found the leadership of the firm too loose and unstructured and too often "invisible." It appeared to me that the Director, though marvelously charismatic, was seen by his staff as spending too much of his time in Washington or at his office at the university or where he could not be reached.

We agreed to spend a full day together in a "confrontation meeting" the following week. The confrontation meeting, invented by Richard Beckhard (1967) (see Volume II of this series), seemed ideally suited to this case. The entire group of 40 professionals along with the Director met in a nearby motel for about seven hours. I spent the first half-hour reviewing recent history and setting forth certain elementary generalizations regarding all human organizations. I set forth certain concepts about organizations which they might find helpful in talking about their own. In the next phase, which lasted one hour, the group of 40 was broken into eight groups of five, cutting across all formal organizational lines, and the participants were asked to discuss the "most significant problems they face in getting their job done. What were the de-motivators? What 'bugged' them?" They were asked to return in one hour with a list of their main problems and causes of those problems. The eight groups brought back dozens of pieces of paper (which were festooned along the walls) listing over 200 problems. I then tried to categorize the problems and came up with five major categories:

1. questions of the identity and destiny of the firm,
2. questions about collaboration and competition,
3. questions about authority, influence, and power,
4. questions about competence, and more precisely doubts about other people's competence, and
5. questions about expectations and clarity, like: who expected what from whom?

Each of the 200 or so problems was numbered from one to five, indicating its particular category. After lunch, the individuals were regrouped according to their formal, intact, organizational structure and were asked to spend an hour or so on recommendations they could make to the Director and top management on the main problems that fell within their particular sphere of influence. The Director and his administrative staff worked together during this period. Finally, in the last period of an hour and a half, the groups reassembled and group by group confronted the Director with their recommendations. To summarize, the day went as follows:

9:30 to 10:00	Introduction
10:00 to 11:00	Data collection—problem generation
11:00 to 12:00	Information sharing and categorization
1:30 to 2:45	Priority setting and action planning
2:45 to 4:30	Confrontation and implementation

To provide a more concrete idea of problems, one group listed the following:

- Meetings like this should start on time. "Minor irritants," like postponed meetings, are rarely communicated to people.

- The authority structure is unclear. Who's my boss? Who judges my work?

- Until recently, there has been little cross-fertilization.

- The Director is inaccessible. Members of the power structure are very accessible to some, but Dr. X (Associate Director) doesn't return his calls. As a result, the number of memos has increased.

- There is no system of setting priorities on distribution of materials. Does a policy exist? Is it possible to have one?

- It is a problem for newcomers to discover who does what in the organization.

- There are too many people employed and then not permitted to exercise the skills they were hired for.

- Too many meetings are held without a specific agenda.

- How do information and decisions that come out of these meetings get communicated?

- Taking over responsibility as acting project director has taken me away from my primary interest—this is irritating and annoying.

- Difficult to get a sure assessment of peoples' strengths and weaknesses.

- Who makes decisions around here?
- Funding is chaotic. Whom do we go to for funds?

The recommendations of the staff to the Director were received, if not gratefully, then without rancor and certainly with great concern. As a result of this meeting, more regular and meaningful meetings were held, a clear-cut organizational structure evolved, and most important, the Director felt that he would much rather spend the bulk of his time on substantive matters and decided to relinquish his role to another person in the firm who had administrative ambition and talent.

Example 4. Data Feedback. Six accounting departments completed surveys concerned with aspects of their organization, work, and human relations. These departments employed about 60 supervisors and 640 nonsupervisory employees. Four of the departments received knowledge of the results of their questionnaires—"feedback"—in conferences over a 12-month period and were called the "experimental departments." The other two "control" departments received no special attention from the management or research group other than the regular administrative practices. Both before and after the experiment in data feedback, these departments filled out lengthy questionnaires which covered a wide variety of attitudes and feelings concerning the major aspects of the work situation. It should be stressed that the "experimental departments" had intensive discussions for almost a year, discussions which were based on surveys they themselves had completed.

When the experimental and control groups were compared, it was found that the groups which experienced the data feedback felt that:

- They were better at getting the job done.
- They were freer to take job problems to their supervisors.
- Their supervisors better understood their point of view.
- Their supervisors got along better with each other.
- They understood better how their supervisor sees things.

As the author of the study (Baumgartel, 1959, p. 6) concluded:

The results of this study suggest that the creative use of new information for conferences and meetings at all levels of departmental organization may be one of the best and most dynamic avenues to management development and organizational growth.

Example 5. Elements in a One-Year Program.   In 1960 a small refinery of about 500 employees with 60 management personnel was on the verge of bankruptcy and practically defunct due to an oversupply of the world's petroleum resources and special production problems of the refinery. The parent firm had all but decided to close the refinery but union and political pressures developed, along with certain changes of policy from headquarters, which led to an attempt to revitalize the refinery. A new top manager was hired and New York headquarters' staff was brought in to help in the organizational development of the refinery.

After a management survey was accomplished, intensive feedback sessions were held with each constituent unit. This was followed by a series of weekly seminars given by prominent organizational theorists whose main purpose was to provide a number of models for thinking about organizational change. Following this, all 60 supervisors participated in a week-long sensitivity training laboratory where the main emphasis was placed on interpersonal competencies and skills in intergroup coordination. As a result of these educational ventures, after which revaluation of needs and rediagnoses were accomplished, a joint committee system for plant-wide participation was achieved along with a modification of the Scanlon labor plan. This was the first time that the Scanlon plan was successfully adapted to a process industry.

Figure 1-1 describes the various steps and strategies followed from the initial exigency of threatened work stoppage to the Scanlon plan.

WHAT IS ORGANIZATION DEVELOPMENT?

On the basis of the foregoing examples we can return to the title of this introductory chapter and rough out the basic characteristics of organization development.

First of all, it is an *educational strategy* adopted to bring about a *planned organizational change.* The strategies differ enormously. In some cases, as in the data feedback example, nothing more complicated than a questionnaire and group discussion is used. In the refinery case, more complex technologies were employed, from fairly elaborate sensitivity training sessions to economic and cost factors. Note also that the point of entry varied. In the State Department case, for example, intergroup relations was viewed as an extremely important strategic leverage point. The Union Carbide and, to a lesser extent, the refinery cases focused on team development. Whatever the strategy, organizational development almost

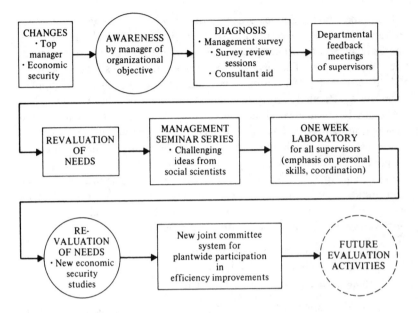

Fig. 1-1 Elements in one-year program in Refinery C.

always concentrates on the values, attitudes, relations, and organizational climate—the "people variable"—as a point of entry rather than on the goals, structure, and technologies of the organization.

This can be best explained by virtue of the fact that the *change agent* is almost always a professional behavioral scientist and would naturally view the human-social aspects of a situation as more comprehensible, if not more accessible and amenable to change. This is, of course, an extremely controversial issue which I will not go into now except to say that there are many (including myself, at times) who believe that other aspects of *client systems* can be more easily and cheaply changed with far better and more reliable results. Nevertheless, organization development, for the most part, takes as its focus of convenience the human side of the enterprise.

The *second* characteristic is that the changes sought for are coupled directly with the *exigency* or demand the organization is trying to cope with. In rare cases, as in the refinery situation, it is a matter of survival; in other, more typical cases, it is a new and rapidly expanding enterprise (like the educational research and development firm) facing a "destination crisis." The tacit issue in the State Department illustration was a changing role for the Foreign Service officer, a role that had to include components of administration, a new and rather vague element, certainly devalued by the Foreign Service officer and equally certain to be pivotal for success in the decade ahead. The organization development cases I have been involved in over the past ten or so years have involved problems of communication (particularly upward), intergroup conflict, leadership issues (particularly problems about succession), questions of identity and destination (almost always due to spectacular growth or technological advances), questions about satisfaction and the ability of the organization to provide adequate and appropriate inducements (particularly for professionals), and questions of organizational effectiveness as measured in the hard indicators of profit, waste, cost, labor turnover—or however effectiveness is measured. In general, all of the above exigencies, and others I have not mentioned, can be grouped into three categories:

1. problems of destiny—growth, identity, and revitalization,
2. problems of human satisfaction and development, and
3. problems of organizational effectiveness.

A *third* characteristic is that organization development relies on an educational strategy which emphasizes *experienced behavior.* Thus, data feedback, sensitivity training, the confrontation meeting, and other experience-based methods are widely used to generate publicly shared data and experience upon which planning and action proceed. To stay with the confrontation meeting for a minute, we see the following steps:

1. generate data relating to exigency,
2. feedback data to relevant groups and people, and
3. plan action on the basis of steps 1 and 2.

Fourth, change agents are for the most part, but not exclusively, *external to the client system.* This is another controversial issue which we need not go into now. There are a few examples of outstanding internal change agents, like Sheldon Davis of TRW Systems or Alfred Marrow of Harwood Manufacturing Company, but generally speaking, certainly during the beginning phases, outside change agents are necessary. This is true for a variety of reasons, not the least of which is the conventional wisdom that an outsider carries more weight. More to the point, I suspect, is that the external consultant can manage to affect—again, especially at first—the power structure in a way that most internal change agents cannot. This again may be related to the aura created by an external (often highly paid) consultant, but it is equally related to the ability of the external change agent to "see" with more innocence and clarity the problems which insiders may have long learned to avoid or overlook and most certainly regard with anxiety. Whatever arguments pro or con can be made with respect to the issue of internal versus external change agents, my own conclusion is that the debate becomes a meaningless one after the beginning (or "unfreezing" stage), but throughout the early phases of any organization development program, an external change agent is deemed essential.

Fifth, organization development implies a *collaborative relationship* between change agent and constituents of the client system. "Collaboration" is a difficult word to do justice to, but it involves mutual trust, joint determination of goals and means, and high mutual influence. In fact, I would be hard put to think of a better set of categories for what is meant by "collaboration" than the ones developed by McGregor and Jones and referred to as "team development" in the first example above.

A *sixth* characteristic is that change agents share a *social philosophy,* a set of values about the world in general and human organizations in particular which shape their strategies, determine their interventions, and largely govern their responses to client systems. More often than not, change agents believe that the realization of these values will ultimately lead not only to a more humane and democratic system but to a more efficient one. What follows is a rough approximation, keeping in mind that there would be important individual differences between change agents, based on their cosmology and competence. Argyris (1962) provides a graphic model which serves as an example. He shows the purported value system which dominates most modern organizations (Fig. 1-2), i.e., bureaucratic values. These values, basically impersonal, task-oriented, and denying humanistic and democratic values, lead to poor, shallow, and mistrustful relationships. They are "phony," nonauthentic relationships and basically incomplete, i.e., they do not permit the natural and free expression of feelings. These nonauthentic relationships lead to a state which Argyris calls "decreased interpersonal competence," a result of the shallow and unevolved relationships. Without interpersonal competence or a "psychologically safe" environment, the organization is a breeding ground for mistrust, intergroup conflict, rigidity, and so on, which in turn lead to a decrease in organizational success in problem-solving.

This is the model: bureaucratic values tend to stress the rational, exclusively task-oriented aspects of work and to ignore the basic human factors which relate to the task and which, if ignored, tend to reduce organizational effectiveness. Managers brought up under this system of values are badly cast to play the intricate human roles now required of them. Their ineptitude and anxieties lead to systems of discord and de-

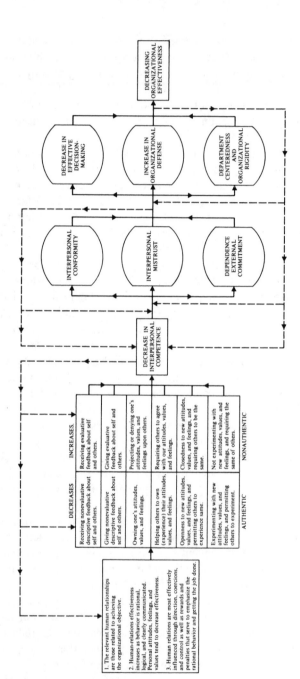

Fig. 1-2 Predominant value system of Organization Development (Argyris, 1962, p. 43).

fense which interfere with the problem-solving capacity of the organization.

The *seventh* characteristic is that change agents share a set of *normative goals* based on their philosophy. The key normative goals can be derived from the social philosophy outlined in the preceding section. Most commonly sought are:

1. Improvement in interpersonal competence.

2. A shift in values so that human factors and feelings come to be considered legitimate.

3. Development of increased understanding between and within working groups in order to reduce tensions.

4. Development of more effective "team management," i.e., the capacity, as in the Union Carbide case, for functional groups to work more competently.

5. Development of better methods of "conflict resolution." Rather than the usual bureaucratic methods which rely mainly on suppression, compromise, and unprincipled power, more rational and open methods of conflict resolution are sought.

6. Development of organic rather than mechanical systems. This is a strong reaction against the idea of organizations as mechanisms which managers "work on," like pushing buttons. Organic systems differ from mechanical systems in the following ways (Table 1-2):

TABLE 1-2

Mechanical Systems	Organic Systems
Exclusive individual emphasis	Relationships between and within groups emphasized
Authority-obedience relationships	Mutual confidence and trust
Delegated and divided responsibility rigidly adhered to	Interdependence and shared responsibility
Strict division of labor and hierarchical supervision	Multigroup membership and responsibility
Centralized decision-making	Wide sharing of responsibility and control
Conflict resolution through suppression, arbitration and/or warfare	Conflict resolution through bargaining or problem-solving

Of course, not all change agents would agree with the foregoing and there would most certainly be many variations on the themes I have been developing. But allowing for important exceptions, most would probably accept the broad value commitments enumerated above. Differences among change agents come into sharper focus in their choice of strategies and educational programs for implementing these normative goals. The subsequent volumes in this series provide concrete examples of the differences which I, possibly too cavalierly, blurred over.

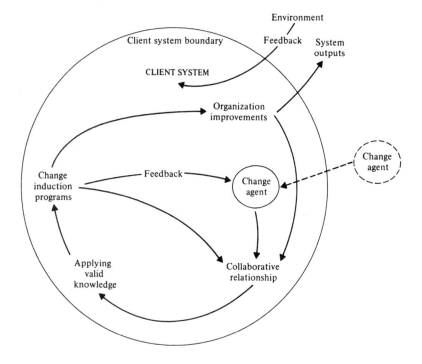

Figure 1-3

Hollis Peter (Bennis and Peter, 1967, p. 317) has developed a graphic model which depicts with amazing simplicity most of the elements I have been describing. Again: an exigency, either internal or external to the organization, stimulates a response by an outside change agent to apply valid knowledge to a client system. These steps lead ultimately (at least in successful cases) to an improvement in system outputs (see Fig. 1-3).

CONCLUSION

In conclusion, it might be useful to say a few words about what organization development *is not*. It should be clear by now that organization development is not simply *sensitivity training*. To be sure, many organization-development practitioners rely to a greater or lesser extent on experience-based educational programs, and some variant of sensitivity training is frequently used. But, as I have tried to show, a wide variety of programs can be effective, from data feedback sessions to confrontation meetings. The important thing about organization development is that data are generated from the client system itself. Frequently, these are the only data that count anyway, as there is sufficient evidence that data collected on "others" (no matter how valid) almost always lack the impact of self-generated data.

I hope it is also clear by now that organization development is not another fancier version of "permissive" leadership. Why this myth continues to be perpetuated despite all the experience to the contrary puzzles me. Organization development does not prescribe any particular "style of leadership" other than an open and confronting one, which is anything but "permissive." Nor does it imply a group consensus as the only form of decision-making, though some writers (such as Blake and Mouton) certainly believe that consensus is a natural conclusion given training under the "Managerial Grid" orientation.

The basic value underlying all organization-development theory and practice is that of *choice*. Through focused attention and through the collection and feedback of relevant data to relevant people, more choices become available and hence better decisions are made. That is essentially what organization development is: an educational strategy employing the widest possible means of experience-based behavior in order to achieve more and better organizational choices in a highly turbulent world.

2

THE BASIC CONDITIONS WHICH CREATE THE NEED FOR ORGANIZATION DEVELOPMENT[1]

The circumstances of an ever-changing market and an ever-changing product are capable of breaking any business organization if that organization is unprepared for change—indeed, in my opinion, if it has not provided procedures for anticipating change.

Alfred P. Sloan

Neither behavioral scientists nor their theories created the need for organization development. They helped, of course, but there should be no doubt that Alfred P. Sloan put his finger on the real cause: *change.* Our social institutions cannot withstand, let alone cope with, the devastating rate of change without fundamental alterations in the way they negotiate their environments and the way they conduct the main operations of their enterprise. Organization development is not something that is "nice" to have around, like a shiny new gadget, or because its value system resembles our Judaic Christian ethic. *Organization development is necessary whenever our social institutions compete for survival under conditions of chronic change.*

The social institution which coordinates the business of almost every human organization we know of—industrial, governmental, educational, investigatory, military, religious, voluntary—is known as *bureaucracy.* As I

1 Most of this chapter is adapted from The Temporary Society, W. E. Bennis and P. E. Slater (New York: Harper, 1968), Chapter 3.

18

refer to it here, bureaucracy is a social invention that was perfected during the industrial revolution to organize and direct the activities of the firm. Under nineteenth century conditions, bureaucracy was an appropriate response, but it is my belief, shared by many practitioners and students of organizational behavior, that this form of organization cannot successfully cope with twentieth century realities. In fact, unless fundamental revision is considered and implemented, organizations will be seriously hampered in reaching their goals, if they survive at all. Organization development is one way that enables management to bring to bear more consciousness of renewal and revitalization so that new and more innovative responses can be developed by organizations facing extraordinary turbulence in the decade ahead.

What follows is a detailed analysis of bureaucracy and why it is peculiarly vulnerable to contemporary conditions. Following that will come an identification of the key human problems facing managerial leadership and the role of organization development in facilitating the necessary evolution toward new forms of organizational life.

Bureaucracy consists of the following components:

1. A well-defined chain of command.

2. A system of procedures and rules for dealing with all contingencies relating to work activities.

3. A division of labor based on specialization.

4. Promotion and selection based on technical competence.

5. Impersonality in human relations.

It is the pyramid arrangement we see on most organizational charts.

The bureaucratic "machine model" was developed as a reaction against the personal subjugation, nepotism, cruelty, and the capricious and subjective judgments which passed for managerial practices during the early days of the industrial revolution. Bureaucracy emerged out of the organizations' need for order and precision and the workers' demands for impartial treatment. It was an organization ideally suited to the values and demands of the Victorian era. And just as bureaucracy emerged as a creative response to a radically new age, so today new organizational designs must be developed.

First I shall try to show why the conditions of our modern industrialized world will bring about the death of bureaucracy. In the second part of this chapter I will suggest a rough model of the organization of the future.

There are at least four relevant threats to bureaucracy:

1. Rapid and unexpected change.

2. Growth in size where the volume of an organization's traditional activities is not enough to sustain growth. (Several factors obtain here: bureaucratic overhead, tighter controls and impersonality due to bureaucratic sprawls, outmoded rules and organizational structures.)

3. Complexity of modern technology where integration between activities and persons of very diverse, highly specialized competence is required.

4. A basically psychological threat springing from a change in managerial behavior.

It might be useful to examine the extent to which these conditions exist right now.

RAPID AND UNEXPECTED CHANGE

Bureaucracy's strength is its capacity to manage efficiently that which is routine and predictable in human affairs. It is almost enough to cite the knowledge and population explosions to raise doubts about its contemporary viability. More revealing, however, are the statistics that demonstrate these overworked phrases:

- Our productivity output per man-hour is now doubling about every 20 years rather than every 40 years, as it did before World War II.

- The Federal government alone spent $16 billion in research and development activities in 1965; it will spend $35 billion by 1980.

- The time lag between a technical discovery and recognition of its commercial uses was 30 years before World War I, 16 years between the wars, and only nine years since World War II.

- In 1946, only 42 cities in the world had populations of more than one million. Today there are 90. In 1930, there were 40 people for each square mile of the earth's land surface. Today there are 63. By the year 2000, it is expected the figure will have soared to 142.

Bureaucracy with its nicely defined chain of command, its rules, and its rigidities is ill-adapted to the rapid change the environment now demands.

GROWTH IN SIZE

While, in theory, there may be no natural limit to the height of a bureaucratic pyramid, in practice the element of complexity is almost invariably introduced with great size. International operation, to cite one significant new element, is the rule rather than exception for most of our biggest corporations. Firms like Standard Oil Company (New Jersey) with more than a hundred foreign affiliates, Mobil Oil Corporation, The National Cash Register Company, Singer Company, Burroughs Corporation, and Colgate-Palmolive Company derive more than half their income or earnings from foreign sales. Many others—such as Eastman Kodak Company, Chas. Pfizer & Company, Inc., Caterpillar Tractor Company, International Harvester Company, Corn Products Company, and Minnesota Mining & Manufacturing Company—make from 30 to 50% of their sales abroad. General Motors Corporation sales are not only nine times those of Volkswagen, they are also bigger than the gross national product of the Netherlands and well over the GNP of a hundred other countries. If we have seen the sun set on the British Empire, we may never see it set on the empires of General Motors, ITT, Shell, and Unilever.[2]

INCREASING DIVERSITY

Today's activities require persons of very diverse, highly specialized competence. Numerous dramatic examples can be drawn from studies of labor markets and job mobility. At some point during the past decade, the United States became the first nation ever to employ more people in service occupations than in the production of tangible goods. Examples of this trend are:

- In the field of education, the *increase* in employment between 1950 and 1960 was greater than the total number employed in the steel, copper, and aluminum industries.
- In the field of health, the *increase* in employment between 1950 and 1960 was greater than the total employment in mining in 1960.

2   Of course, size alone will not necessarily lead to the end of bureaucratic machinery—witness the Federal government. But, even there, the mounting size and scope is leading to a neo-Jeffersonian approach with increasing responsibility sequestered by state and local agencies.

These changes, plus many more that are harder to demonstrate statistically, break down the old, industrial trend toward more and more people doing either simple or undifferentiated chores.

Hurried growth, rapid change, and increase in specialization—pit these three factors against the five components of the pyramid structure described earlier, and we should expect the pyramid of bureaucracy to begin crumbling.

CHANGE IN MANAGERIAL BEHAVIOR

There is, I believe, a subtle but perceptible change in the philosophy underlying management behavior. Its magnitude, nature, and antecedents, however, are shadowy because of the difficulty of assigning numbers. (Whatever else statistics do for us, they provide a welcome illusion of certainty.) Nevertheless, real change seems under way because of:

1. A new concept of *man* based on increased knowledge of his complex and shifting needs, which replaces an oversimplified, innocent, push-button idea of man.

2. A new concept of *power,* based on collaboration and reason, which replaces a model of power based on coercion and threat.

3. A new concept of *organizational values,* based on humanistic-democratic ideals, which replaces the depersonalized, mechanistic value system of bureaucracy.

The primary cause of this shift in management philosophy stems not from the bookshelf but from managers themselves. Many of the behavioral scientists, like Douglas McGregor or Rensis Likert, have clarified and articulated—even legitimized—what managers have only half registered to themselves. I am convinced, for example, that the popularity of McGregor's book, *The Human Side of Enterprise,* was based on his rare empathy for a vast audience of managers who are wistful for an alternative to the mechanistic concept of authority, i.e., he outlined a vivid utopia of more authentic human relationships than most organizational practices today allow. Furthermore, I suspect that the desire for relationships in business has little to do with a profit motive per se, though it is often rationalized as doing so. The real push for these changes stems from the need, not only to humanize the organization, but to use it as a crucible of personal growth and the development of self-realization.[3]

Another aspect of this shift in values has to do with man's historical quest for self-awareness, for using reason to achieve and stretch his potentialities, his possibilities. This deliberate self-analysis has spread to large and more complex social systems—organizations where there has been a dramatic upsurge of this spirit of inquiry over the past two decades. At new depths and over a wider range of affairs, organizations are opening their operations to self-inquiry and self-analysis, which involves a change in how the men who make history and the men who make knowledge regard each other. The scientists have realized their affinity with men of affairs, and the latter have found a new receptivity and respect for men of knowledge.

I am calling this new development "organizational revitalization," a complex social process which involves a deliberate and self-conscious examination of organizational behavior and a collaborative relationship between managers and scientists to improve performance. For many this new form of collaboration can be taken for granted. I have simply regarded reciprocity between the academician and manager as inevitable and natural. But I can assure you that this development is unprecedented, that never before in history, in any society, has man in his organizational context so willingly searched, scrutinized, examined, inspected, or contemplated—for meaning, for purpose, for improvement.

This shift in outlook has taken a good deal of courage from both partners in this encounter. The manager has had to shake off old prejudices about "eggheads" and "long-hair" intellectuals. More important, the manager has had to make himself and his organization vulnerable and receptive to external sources and to new, unexpected, even unwanted information. The academician, on the other hand, has had to shed some of his natural hesitancies. Scholarly conservatism is admirable except as something to hide behind, and for a long time caution was a defense against reality.

3   Let me propose an hypothesis to explain this tendency. It rests on the assumption that man has a basic need for transcendental experiences, somewhat like the psychological rewards that William James claimed religion provided—"an assurance of safety and a temper of peace, and, in relation to others, a preponderance of loving affections." Can it be that as religion has become secularized, less transcendental, men search for substitutes such as close interpersonal relationships, psychoanalysis—even the release provided by drugs such as LSD?

It might be useful to dwell a bit longer on the role of academic man and his growing involvement with social action, using the field of management education as a case in point. Until recently, the field of business was unknown to, or snubbed by, the academic establishment. There, management education and research were at best regarded with dark suspicion as if contact with the world of reality—particularly monetary reality—was equivalent to a dreadful form of pollution.

In fact, historically, academic man has taken one of two stances toward "the establishment," any establishment: that of a rebellious critic or of a withdrawn snob. The stance of the rebel is currently popular. Witness the proliferation of such paperback titles as: *The Power Elite, The Lonely Crowd, Organization Man, The Hidden Persuaders, Tyranny of Testing, Mass Leisure, Exurbanites, Death and Life of Great American Cities, The American Way of Death, Compulsory Mis-Education, The Status Seekers, Growing Up Absurd, The Paper Economy, Silent Spring, Child Worshippers, The Affluent Society,* and *Depleted Society.*

The withdrawn stance can still be observed in some of our American universities, but less so these days. However, it continues to be the prevailing attitude in many European universities. There the universities seem intent on preserving the monastic ethos of their medieval origins, offering a lulling security to their inmates, and sapping the curriculum of virility and relevance. Max Beerbohm's (1966, p. 126) whimsical and idyllic fantasy of Oxford, *Zuleika Dobson,* dramatizes this:

It is the mild, miasmal air, not less than the grey beauty and the gravity of the buildings that has helped Oxford to produce and foster, externally, her peculiar race of artist-scholars, scholar-artists. . . . The Buildings and their traditions keep astir in his mind whatsoever is gracious; the climate enfolding and enfeebling him, lulling him, keeps him careless of the sharp, harsh exigent realities of the outerworld. These realities may be seen by him. . . . But they cannot fire him. Oxford is too damp for that.

"Adorable Dreamer," said Matthew Arnold, in his valedictory to Oxford:

Adorable dreamer, whose heart has been so romantic! who has given thyself so prodigally, given thyself to sides and to heroes not mine, only never to the Philistine! . . . what teacher could ever so save us from that bondage to which we are all prone . . . the bondage of what binds us all, the narrow, the mundane, the merely practical.

The intellectual and the manager have only recently come out of hiding and recognized the enormous possiblities of joint ventures. Remember that the idea of the professional school is new, even in the case of the venerable threesome—law, medicine, and engineering—to say nothing of recent upstarts like business and public administration. It is as new as the institutionalization of science itself, say around 50 years. And even today, this change is not greeted with unmixed joy. Colin Clark, the economist, writing in a recent issue of the magazine *Encounter,* referred to the "dreadful suggestion that Oxford ought to have a business school."

It is probably true that in the United States we have had a more pragmatic attitude toward knowledge than anywhere else. Many observers have been impressed with the disdain European intellectuals seem to show for practical matters. Even in Russia, where one would least expect it, there is little interest in the "merely useful." Harrison Salisbury, of the *New York Times,* was struck during his recent travels in the Soviet Union by the almost total absence of liaison between research and practical application. He saw only one agricultural experimental station on the American model. There, professors were working in the fields and told him, "People call us Americans."

There may not be many American professors working in the fields, but they can be found, when not waiting in airports, almost everywhere else: in factories, in government, in less advanced countries, and more recently, in backward areas of our own country, in mental hospitals, in the State Department, in practically all the institutional crevices PhD candidates can worm their way into. They are advising, counseling, researching, recruiting, interpreting, developing, consulting, training, and working for the widest variety of clients imaginable. This is not to say that the deep ambivalence some Americans hold toward the intellectual has disappeared, but it does indicate that academic man has become more committed to action, in greater numbers, with more diligence, and with higher aspirations than at any other time in history.

Indeed, Fritz Machlup, the economist, has coined a new economic category called the "knowledge industry," which, he claims, accounts for 29% of the gross national product. Clark Kerr (1964, p. 86), the former president of the University of California, said not too long ago:

What the railroads did for the second half of the last century and the automobile did for the first half of this century may be done for the second half of this century by the knowledge industry: that is, to serve as the focal point of national growth. And the university is at the center of the knowledge process.

TABLE 2-1. Human Problems Confronting Contemporary Organizations

Problem	Bureaucratic Solutions	New Twentieth-Century Conditions
Integration		
Integrating individual needs and organizational goals.	No solution because there is no problem. Individual vastly over-simplified, regarded as passive instrument. Tension between personality and role disregarded.	Emergence of human sciences and understanding of man's complexity. Rising aspirations. Humanistic-democratic ethos.
Social Influence		
Distributing power and sources of power and authority.	An explicit reliance on legal-rational power, but an implicit usage of coercive power. In any case, a confused, ambiguous, shifting complex of competence, coercion, and legal code.	Separation of management from ownership. Rise of trade unions and general education. Negative and unin-tended effects of authoritarian rule.
Collaboration		
Producing mechanisms for the control of conflict.	The "rule of hierarchy" to resolve conflicts between ranks and the "rule of coordination" to resolve conflict between horizontal groups. Loyalty.	Specialization and professionalization and increased need for interdependence. Leadership too complex for one-man rule or omniscience.

Problem	Bureaucratic Solutions	New Twentieth-Century Conditions
Adaptation		
Responding appropriately to changes induced by the environment.	Environment stable, simple, and predictable; tasks routine. Adapting to change occurs in haphazard and adventitious ways. Unanticipated consequences abound.	External environment of firm more turbulent, less predictable. Unprecedented rate of technological change.
Identity		
Achieving clarity, consensus, and commitment to organizational goals.	Primary goal of organization clear, simple, and stable.	Increased complexity due to diversity, multipurpose capability, intersector mobility. Creates role complexity, conflict, and ambiguity.
Revitalization		
Dealing with growth and decay.	Underlying assumption that the future will be certain and at least basically similar to the past.	Rapid changes in technologies, tasks, manpower, raw materials, norms and values of society, goals of enterprise and society all make constant attention to the process of revision imperative.

PROBLEMS CONFRONTED IN ORGANIZATION DEVELOPMENT

The core problems confronting any organization can be categorized into six major areas. First, let us consider the problems, then let us see how our twentieth-century conditions of constant change have made the bureaucratic approach to these problems obsolete. This is summarized in Table 2-1. We start with the problem of how man's needs can be fused with the needs and goals of his employing organization.

Integration

The problem is how to integrate individual needs and organizational goals. In other words, it is the inescapable conflict between individual needs (like spending time with the family) and organizational demands (like meeting deadlines).

Under twentieth-century conditions of constant change there has been an emergence of human sciences and a deeper understanding of man's complexity. Today, integration encompasses the entire range of issues concerned with incentives, rewards, and motivations of the individual and how the organization succeeds or fails in adjusting to these issues. In our society, where personal attachments play an important role, the individual is appreciated, and there is genuine concern for his well-being, not just in a veterinary-hygiene sense, but as a moral, integrated personality.

The problem of integration, like most human problems, has a venerable past. The modern version goes back at least 160 years and was precipitated by an historical paradox: the twin births of modern individualism and modern industrialism. The former brought about a deep concern for and a passionate interest in the individual and his personal rights. The latter brought about increased mechanization of organized activity. Competition between the two has intensified as each decade promises more freedom and hope for man and more stunning achievements for technology. I believe that our society *has* opted for more humanistic and democratic values, however unfulfilled they may be in practice. It will "buy" these values even at loss in efficiency because it feels it can now afford the loss.

Social Influence

This problem is essentially one of power and of how power is distributed. It is a complex issue and alive with controversy, partly because of an ethical component and partly because studies of leadership and power distribution can be interpreted in many ways, and almost always in ways that coincide with one's biases (including a cultural leaning toward democracy).

The problem of power has to be seriously reconsidered because of dramatic situational changes that make the possiblity of one-man rule not necessarily "bad," but impractical. I refer to changes in top management's role.

Peter Drucker (1954, p. 167) listed 41 major responsibilities of the chief executive and declared that "90 percent of the trouble we are having with the chief executive's job is rooted in our superstition of the one-man chief." Many factors make one-man control obsolete, among them: the broadening product base of industry, the impact of new technology, the scope of international operation, the separation of management from ownership, the rise of trade unions, and the dissemination of general education. The real power of the chief has been eroding in most organizations even though both he and the organization cling to the older concept.

Collaboration

This is the problem of managing and resolving conflicts. Bureaucratically, it grows out of the very same social process of conflict and stereotyping that has divided nations and communities. As organizations become more complex, they fragment and divide, building tribal patterns and symbolic codes, which often work to exclude others (secrets and jargon, for example) and on occasion to exploit differences for inward (and always fragile) harmony.

Recent research is shedding new light on the problem of conflict. Psychologist Robert R. Blake in his stunning experiments has shown how simple it is to induce conflict, how difficult to arrest it. He takes two groups of people who have never before been together, gives them a task which will be judged by an impartial jury. In less than an hour, each group devolves into a tightly knit band with all the symptoms of an in group. They regard their product as a "masterwork" and the other group's as commonplace at best. "Other" becomes "enemy." "We are good, they are bad; we are right, they are wrong." (Blake and Mouton, 1964).

Jaap Rabbie (1966), conducting experiments on intergroup conflict at the University of Utrecht, has been amazed by the ease with which conflict and stereotype develop. He brings into an experimental room two groups and distributes green name tags and pens to one group, red pens and tags to the other. The two groups do not compete; they do not even interact. They are only in sight of each other while they silently complete a questionnaire. Only ten minutes are needed to activate defensiveness and fear, reflected in the hostile and irrational perceptions of both "reds" and "greens."

In a recent essay on animal behavior, Harvard professor Erik Erikson develops the idea of "pseudo-species." Pseudo species act as if they were separate species created at the beginning of time by supernatural intent. He argues (1965):

Man has evolved (by whatever kind of evolution and for whatever adaptive reasons) in pseudo-species, i.e., tribes, clans, classes, etc. Thus, each develops not only a distinct sense of identity but also a conviction of harboring *the* human identity, fortified against other pseudo-species by prejudices which mark them as extraspecific and inimical to "genuine" human endeavor. Paradoxically, however, newly born man is (to use Ernst Mayr's term) a generalist creature who could be made to fit into any number of pseudo-species and must, therefore, become "specialized during a prolonged childhood.". . .

Modern organizations abound with pseudo-species, bands of specialists held together by the illusion of a unique identity and with a tendency to view other pseudo-species with suspicion and mistrust.

Adaptation

The real *coup de grâce* to bureaucracy has come as much from the turbulent environment as from its incorrect assumptions about human behavior. The pyramidal structure of bureaucracy, where power was concentrated at the top—perhaps by one person who had the knowledge and resources to control the entire enterprise—seemed perfect to run a railroad. And undoubtedly, for tasks like building railroads, for the routinized tasks of the nineteenth and early twentieth centuries, bureaucracy was and is an eminently suitable social arrangement.

Today, due primarily to the growth of science, technology, and research and development activities, the organizational environment of organizations is rapidly changing. It is a turbulent environment, not a placid and predictable one, and there is a deepening interdependence among the economic and other facets of society. This means the economic organizations are increasingly enmeshed in legislation and public policy. Put more simply, it means that the government will be more involved, more of the time. It may also mean, and this is radical, that maximizing cooperation rather than competition between organizations—particularly if their fates are correlated (which is most certainly to be common)—may become a strong possibility.

Identity

Organizations never refer to it as such, but they are as susceptible to identity crises as adolescents. College students seem to recover from theirs shortly after graduation, whereas organizations are never fully "cured" and may re-experience the anxiety at different phases of organizational development. When an individual is vague, mixed-up, and uncertain about who he is or where he is going, we call it "identity diffusion." An identity crisis can be experienced as well when an individual experiences constriction of choice and possibilities.

In organizations, the problem of identity has many of the same properties as "diffusion" and "constraint," but most often it is discussed in terms of the degree to which the organization is clear about and committed to its goals. Modern organizations are extremely vulnerable to an identity problem for many of the reasons discussed earlier, but chiefly because rapid growth and turbulence transform and distort the original, more simplified goals. An organization, for example, attains riches and fame for an invention and then discovers it is in the business of production without ever truly deciding on that. A university sets out purely and simply to transmit knowledge to students, but suddenly finds that 50% of its budget comes from government research grants and finds itself part of the defense industry.

What makes matters worse is the fact that organizational complexity and diversity lead to differing orientations within subsystems so that goals that may be clear and identified within one part of the organization are antithetical, or at best only vaguely understood, by other subsystems of the organization.

Constant surveillance of the primary tasks is a necessity, particularly if the organization is embedded in a dynamic, protean environment.

Revitalization

This is the problem of growth and decay. As Alfred North Whitehead has said:

The art of free society consists first in the maintenance of the symbolic code, and secondly, in the fearlessness of revision. . . . Those societies which cannot combine reverence to their symbols with freedom of revision must ultimately decay. . . ."

Growth and decay emerge as the penultimate conditions of contemporary society. Organizations, as well as societies, must be concerned with those social structures that engender buoyancy, resilience, and a fearlessness of revision.

I introduce the term "revitalization" to embrace all the social mechanisms that stagnate and regenerate, as well as the process of this cycle. The elements of revitalization are:

1. An ability to learn from experience and to codify, store, and retrieve the relevant knowledge.

2. An ability to learn how to learn, that is, to develop methods for improving the learning process.

3. An ability to acquire and use feedback mechanisms on performance, in short, to be self-analytical.

4. An ability to direct one's own destiny.

These qualities have a good deal in common with what John Gardner calls "self-renewal." For the organization, it means conscious attention to its own evolution. Without a planned methodology and explicit direction, the enterprise will not realize its potential.

Integration, distribution of power, collaboration, adaptation, identity, and *revitalization*—these are the major human problems of the next 25 years. How organizations cope with and manage these tasks will undoubtedly determine the viability of the enterprise.

DETERMINANT CONDITIONS

Against this background I should like to set forth some of the conditions that will dictate organizational life in the next two or three decades.

The Environment

Rapid technological change and diversification will lead to more and more partnerships between government and business. It will be a truly mixed economy. Because of the immensity and expense of the projects, there will be fewer identical units competing in the same markets and organizations will become more interdependent.

The four main features of this environment are:

1. Interdependence rather than competition.
2. Turbulence and uncertainty rather than readiness and certainty.
3. Large-scale rather than small-scale enterprises.
4. Complex and multinational rather than simple national enterprises.

Population Characteristics

The most distinctive characteristic of our society is education. It will become even more so. Within 15 years, two-thirds of our population living in metropolitan areas will have attended college. Adult education is growing even faster, probably because of the rate of professional obsolescence. The Killian report showed that the average engineer required further education only ten years after getting his degree. It will be almost routine for the experienced physician, engineer, and executive to go back to school for advanced training every two or three years. All of this education is not just "nice." It is necessary.

One other characteristic of the population which will aid our understanding of organizations of the future is increasing job mobility. The ease of transportation, coupled with the needs of a dynamic environment, change drastically the ideas of owning a job or having roots. Already 20% of our population change their mailing address at least once a year.

Work Values

The increased level of education and mobility will change the values we place on work. People will be more intellectually committed to their jobs and will probably require more involvement, participation, and autonomy.

Also, people will be more "other-oriented," taking cues for their norms and values from their immediate environment rather than tradition.

Tasks and Goals

The tasks of the organization will be more technical, complicated, and unprogrammed. They will rely on intellect instead of muscle. And they will be too complicated for one person to comprehend, to say nothing of control. Essentially, they will call for the collaboration of specialists in a project or a team form of organization.

There will be a complication of goals. Business will increasingly concern itself with its adaptive or innovative-creative capacity. In addition, supragoals will have to be articulated, goals that shape and provide the foundation for the goal structure. For example, one might be a system for detecting new and changing goals; another could be a system for deciding priorities among goals.

Finally, there will be more conflict and contradiction among diverse standards for organizational effectiveness. This is because professionals tend to identify more with the goals of their profession than with those of their immediate employer. University professors can be used as a case in point. Their inside work may be a conflict between teaching and research, while more of their income is derived from outside sources such as foundations and consultant work. They tend to be poor company men because they divide their loyalty between their professional values and organizational goals.

Organization

The social structure of organizations of the future will have some unique characteristics. The key word will be "temporary." There will be adaptive, rapidly changing *temporary* systems. These will be task forces organized around problems to be solved by groups of relative strangers with diverse professional skills. The group will be arranged on an organic rather than mechanical model; it will evolve in response to a problem rather than to programmed role expectations. The executive thus becomes coordinator or "linking pin" between various task forces. He must be a man who can speak the polyglot jargon of research, with skills to relay information and to mediate between groups. People will be evaluated not according to rank but according to skill and professional training. Organizational charts will consist of project groups rather than stratified functional groups. (This trend is already visible in the aerospace and construction industries, as well as in many professional and consulting firms.)

Adaptive, problem-solving, temporary systems of diverse specialists, linked together by coordinating and task-evaluating executive specialists in an organic flux—this is the organizational form that will gradually replace bureaucracy as we know it. As no catchy phrase comes to mind, I call these new-style organizations "*adaptive* structures." Organizational arrangements of this sort may not only reduce the intergroup conflicts mentioned earlier; they may also induce honest-to-goodness creative collaboration.

Motivation

Adaptive organizations should increase motivation and thereby effectiveness, because they create conditions under which the individual can gain increased satisfaction with the task itself. Thus, there should be harmony between the educated individual's need for tasks that are meaningful, satisfying, and creative *and* an adaptive organizational structure.

Accompanying the increased integration between individual and organizational goals, will be new modes of relating and changing commitments to work groups. Most of the research on the individual's relationship to his peer group at work indicates the significance of the work group on performance and morale. The work group creates and reinforces norms and standards, from the appropriate number of units produced to the appropriate amount of interaction and intimacy. The significance of the work group for the communication, control, and regulation of behavior cannot be overestimated. But in the new adaptive organizations I am talking about, work groups will be temporary systems, which means that people will have to learn to develop quick and intense relationships on the job and learn to bear the absence of more enduring work relationships. Thus we should expect to experience a concentration of emotional energy in forming relationships quickly and intensely and then a dissolution and rapid relocation of personal attachments. From an organizational point of view we can expect that more time and energy will have to be spent on continual rediscovery of the appropriate mix of people, competencies, and tasks within an ambiguous and unstructured existence.

I think that the future I describe is not necessarily a "happy" one. Coping with rapid change, living in temporary work systems, developing meaningful relations and then breaking them—all augur social strains and psychological tensions. Teaching how to live with ambiguity, to identify with the adaptive process, to make a virtue out of contingency, and to be self-directing—these will be the tasks of education, the goals of maturity, and the achievement of the successful individual.

CONCLUSION

In conclusion, I hope I have been able to persuade the reader that we must anticipate and shape a number of profound changes in the ways we organize our work and human relations. Though some changes are seen as "inevitable" given certain trends (such as industrialization, complexity, and scale) we have little choice, so it seems, to participate in the development of more humane and democratic systems. That's what organization development is all about, and that's why it has emerged as such a zestful avenue for revitalization in the late 1960's.

3

QUESTIONS AND ANSWERS: ORGANIZATION DEVELOPMENT

PART I: THE PROFESSIONALS

Several months ago I was asked to speak to a small group of psychiatrists on the topic of organization development, and it was decided by the chairman of the group to use a question and answer format. The group devoted several hours to reading some of my writings as well as those of others in the field and to formulating questions which they would put to me in person. Unfortunately, the session was not recorded, but the questions, I think, provide a useful way to get at what most people want to know about organization development. So, without further background, here are the questions (as posed by the group) and my answers to those questions, as memory permits.

Q.: Discuss briefly the assumptions, interventions, and goals of change agents in organization development.

A.: I'll start with *goals*. There is more or less agreement about them:

1. To create an open, problem-solving climate throughout an organization.

2. To supplement the authority associated with role or status with the authority of knowledge and competence.

3. To locate decision-making and problem-solving responsibilities as close to the information sources as possible.

4. To build trust among persons and groups throughout an organization.

5. To make competition more relevant to work goals and to maximize collaborative efforts.

6. To develop a reward system which recognizes both the achievement of the organization's goals (profits or service) and development of people.

7. To increase the sense of "ownership" of organization objectives throughout the work force.

8. To help managers to manage according to relevant objectives rather than according to "past practices" or according to objectives which do not make sense for one's area of responsibility.

9. To increase self-control and self-direction for people within the organization.

I touched on many of the *assumptions* of organization development in the first chapter of this volume, so I will not dwell on them now except to say that the assumptions about individuals are generally hopeful: that most individuals, we assume, want to grow and develop, that individuals tend to fight or resist significant changes that they had no part in developing, that most individuals require a suitable human group to identify with, and that most individuals react in "neighborly ways," if I can use that old-fashioned phrase, when they feel unthreatened and have high self-esteem.

The *assumptions* I would make about organizations derive from the preceding chapter. Organizational systems, like other organisms, evolve and have a life cycle. They have a dawn and, quite often in recent years, a sudden old age or stagnation period. Given the pace of events and the turbulent environment, organizations confront tremendous problems if decline is not inevitable. Essentially, this means that organizational systems must renew themselves continuously if they are to survive in this society.

About *interventions*, I described some of them in Chapter 1, and other volumes in this series go into great detail. A list of the most common interventions follows:

1. Discrepancy. This intervention calls attention to a contradiction in action or attitudes. This kind of confrontation is useful for keeping the organization on a new course, rather than allowing it to shift unwittingly into old and less satisfactory behavior patterns owing to momentary pressures.

2. Theory. A second kind of intervention occurs where a confrontation draws on behavioral-science concepts and theory to throw into bold relief the connection between underlying assumptions and present behavior. In addition, theory sometimes can be useful in predicting the consequences likely to follow from embarking on any specialized course of action.

3. Procedural. This intervention provides a critique of how various steps of effort in organization development activities may or may not aid problem-solving.

4. Relationship. This kind of intervention focuses attention of participants on issues which arise between people as they work together. It is needed to reduce or to eliminate interpersonal frictions. With this focus of attention on personal feelings, particularly strong negative tensions which hinder coordinated effort, emotions can be examined and resolved.

5. Experimentation. Another intervention involves experimentation which permits testing and comparing two or more courses of action *before* a final decision is taken, particularly when the way to proceed has become institutionalized or tradition-bound.

6. Dilemma. A dilemma intervention, which aids in accurately identifying a choice point in managerial actions, often can help members reexamine outworn assumptions and search for alternatives other than those under consideration.

7. Perspective. Many times, in the intensity of the effort applied in production settings, it seems inevitable that individuals or teams will lose their sense of direction. Thereafter, it is increasingly difficult to reestablish a course of action which can move the situation away from momentary problem-solving toward larger issues. A perspective intervention permits present actions to be evaluated by providing a background of broader historical orientation.

8. Organization Structure. It is possible to think of many organization development efforts which leave the very structure of the organization unevaluated and unexamined. Students of organization change are correct in pointing out that many causes of organizational ineffectiveness are not found in procedures or team effectiveness or even in the absence of performance goals. Rather, the fabric of the organization itself can prevent communication, decision-making, and the application of effort from being as effective as it might be under different organizational arrangements. An organizational intervention focuses on issues which confront the total organization membership or its various subcomponents.

9. *Cultural.* A "cultural" intervention examines traditions, precedents, and established practices which constitute properties of the organizational fabric itself. Challenging the appropriateness of organization culture is difficult, because it permeates actions in such a silent way. Yet, the great challenge is to bring organization culture under deliberate management. The intervention which lifts up culture for examination may indeed be one of the most critical of all.

Q.: We want to spend most of this session getting a concrete idea of how you operate as a change agent. Could you begin your exposition by giving us a brief overview of a typical consultation in which you have recently been involved?

A.:   Here is an example of an ongoing organization development program at a major American corporation:[1]

The president and division vice presidents of the organization began a series of extended semiannual meetings for intensive review and planning in relation to their own team functioning and the progress of the entire corporation. At the same time, the vice presidents were given the opportunity to begin divisional development projects.

In one division, an outside consultant interviewed the vice president and his 13 department directors to survey organizational needs. The problems uncovered ranged from "not enough hardware to do the job" to fierce distrust of the vice president. ("If I have a problem he'll never know about it," one said.) The vice president's major concern was that he never seemed to know what was going on—the reports he received didn't seem to match what he observed as he toured the various operations.

The consultant categorized the presented problems and reported them at a meeting of the entire group. After the group validated the problems, they sorted them according to the kinds of resources needed to solve them, then chose those which they would begin to work on.

The directors confronted the vice president on the problems created by his style of communication and began a process which has led to significant changes in the communication structure and pattern.

Concern about the relevance and openness of monthly staff meetings has led to shared responsibility for the meetings. Each director takes responsibility for planning a session and uses the consultant to help him learn how to design and conduct meetings.

1   From "What is OD?" (1968).

Traditionally, the division had simply boxed off and bypassed an executive whose work was inadequate. Now, through a process of individual interviews and group discussions, the division is beginning to take the approach that it can recover people by taking a positive, creative look at individual and organizational needs. Through a similar process, the division is developing a new procedure aimed at reducing the interdepartmental stress generated by the organization's method of allocating overhead.

The group continually evaluates its developmental progress, but it also conducts a more formal appraisal of the development programs, and of its use of its consultants, at six-month intervals. It has now achieved enough mutual commitment and enough mastery of everyday processes so that it can actually work on a long-held goal: looking to organizational needs five and ten years from now and beginning to plan for inevitable organizational change.

This capacity to deal with both everyday and long-term issues, with both individuals and organizational dynamics, is the essence of a self-renewing organization and the goal of organization development.

Q.: With this case as illustrative material, could you tell us how you get your initial consultation invitation? At what stage do you discuss the terms of your service? How much do you find out about the organization before you go in? Do you sign a contract? At what stage? What is the contract like? How do you fix your fee?

A.: You must understand at the outset that organization development itself is a new profession and has not fully, or by any means systematically, set out its ethical posture *vis-à-vis* clients as the more mature professions have. It is only recently, in fact, that the behavioral sciences have accustomed themselves to a lay clientèle, and there are many ambiguities here, because of not only the newness itself, but the profound difference in the nature of the client, a complex human system, that transcends the usual boundaries of practice. In short, complexity abounds when you deal, as a practitioner, with a system (organization, community, society) instead of an individual.

In order to be more concrete, I have asked an esteemed colleague if he would agree to reprint a letter he wrote to a potential client just before actually beginning as a consultant. My colleague spent a day or so talking with the President of the company and several other top executives and then wrote the following letter.

Dear Ralph,

In line with preliminary conversations held with you and Mr. Jones, I would like to propose the following arrangements for consultation during the next 12 month period.

1. That you employ my services to aid in the development of a management development program for ABC. The steps in such a program cannot as yet be specified in detail but would involve some of the following:

   a. A series of meetings between yourself, some key internal people concerned with the problem, and myself for the purpose of laying out a detailed plan of action.

   b. Review and discussion of the plan of action by a top management group. Part of such meetings would be to develop, review, and test some basic goals for any management development effort. I should probably meet with the group to act as a resource in such discussions.

   c. Development of a plan to involve present supervision in a diagnostic program to determine the concrete goals toward which a development effort should be directed.

   d. Based on the diagnosis reached in steps b and c develop actual program components and build them gradually into the system.

2. My role in these activities would undoubtedly be a multiple one but would focus on being a procedural catalyst and content resource, i.e., helping you set up a system for gathering data, making plans, and implementing decisions, bringing in knowledge from other companies, research studies, etc., as appropriate.

3. My point of contact or "client" should be you alone or some group of which you are a part. Work with others would then be coordinated through this group.

4. My standard consulting fee is a per diem rate of $300.00. This rate is based on comparable consulting done with other companies. Incidentally, the above information about companies must be kept confidential since these involve current relationships and I have not cleared with them the quotation of rates.

5. I would estimate that the above steps can be implemented over the course of a year, though the actual running of programs would of

course vary in terms of when to start them, for how long to run them, etc. It would be my assumption, however, that major gains will derive from the planning process itself.

6. I would propose that my time be budgeted at an average of 2 to 3 days per month or a total of 30 days for the coming year, subject to review at any time as the needs of the program may increase or decrease.

If the above conditions seem acceptable, I would propose we spend the morning of July 8 formulating some plans.

Sincerely,

Jack Brown
Professor of
Organizational Psychology

Whether or not this letter is typical may not be important, but it does represent the "terms of reference" for one extremely experienced and mature organization development consultant, teaching at a university. His approach tends to corroborate my own experience, and the lessons we can learn from this one example may raise a number of discussion points. First of all, organization development service is a personalized operation. You will not find a listing of organization development in the "yellow pages." This means essentially that a few individuals throughout the country, primarily though not exclusively based in universities, are invited by organizations to help. Usually, a colleague who cannot add another consultation to his load asks a respected colleague to help out. The "contract," if it can be called that, is informal and mostly oral. Neither the consultant nor the client is too certain at this stage as to the causes and cures of the problem, so the "contract" is left specifically vague. As to fees, they vary tremendously. For a topflight organization development man, I suspect that now—for the top 1%—the fee would be between $300 and $400 per day. The average competent organization development practitioner charges somewhere around $200 per day. I should add, however, that both the most and least experienced organization development practitioner arrives at a lower fee if the relationship is a continuing one.[2]

---

2   And I should add that in some cases, the consultant may accept far lower fees, particularly if the client system is particularly interesting or if research is involved or if the client is poor.

The organization development network is an amazingly close one, and in every city just about everyone knows the other members and their distinctive competencies. I occasionally refer interested clients to NTL (1201 Sixteenth Street, N.W., Washington, D.C.) for competent organization development practitioners if the prospective client needs help in identifying organization development staff.

Q.: What are your first steps in clarifying the consultation problem? How do you define the boundaries of the client system? What sanctions do you need from what levels of the organization before you agree to act as a consultant? Have you ever refused an invitation to engage in organization development?

A.: I stick fairly close to the approach that my colleague (reported in the letter above) used, that is, I enter a relationship on the basis that neither the client nor I know what the underlying problems are and that I need to explore and get a "feel" for the situation before committing myself fully to the client system and before it fully entrusts itself to me. All we have at the outset is a mutually accepted and vague goal that organizational improvement is important to work for and is possible.

In making my initial reconnaissance I very often talk at length with most of the key people about what seems to be at the forefront of their minds, their problems, their human concerns, their hopes for the organization, and what seems to block the fulfillment of their hopes. I also try to observe as many meetings as I can so that I can observe how people relate to one another, how decisions are made, and to acquire a perspective that interviews alone cannot provide.

There are many reasons for what may seem to you an inordinate amount of time talking with people and observing meetings. First of all, it is essential to the organization development consultant that he acquaint himself as much as possible with the people, products, process, and environment of the client. Second, his presence legitimizes his role and communicates an official acceptance. Third, it is imperative that the very top of the organization—or the very top of the division or unit within which the organizational development program takes place—is committed to the goals and strategies of organization development. Without this clear understanding and commitment by the top leadership, the program may be too vulnerable to the rather natural ups and downs of any change program. I will have more to say about this later on, but I cannot overstate the importance of a hierarchical umbrella of acceptance if the organization development program is to succeed.

It may be useful at this point to state some of the conditions that are essential to a successful organization development program in a more systematic way. Some years ago, my colleague Edgar Schein (Schein and Bennis, 1965) wrote a book which included a section on conditions of the client system that would have to be considered before initiating an organization development program. What follows is an abridged and slightly revised version of that chapter.

CONSIDERATION FOR THE SUCCESSFUL ADOPTION OF ORGANIZATION DEVELOPMENT BY ORGANIZATIONS

In this section we will examine the state of the client system or subsystem as it concerns the successful adoption of organization development. In considering the state of the client system or subsystem,[3] a number of questions must be asked:

1. Are the learning goals of organization development appropriate?

2. Is the cultural state of the client system ready for organization development?

3. Are the key people involved?

4. Are members of the client system adequately prepared and oriented to organization development?

1. Are the learning goals of organization development appropriate? To what extent do the goals relate to the effectiveness of the client system?

We can think of many client systems where the answer to these questions may be negative owing to market, technological, and competitive conditions. Serious attention must be given, particularly in the early stages, to the appropriateness of organization development change goals for the particular client system. A great deal of effort, at first, must be directed to diagnosing the client system's needs in relation to the anticipated outcomes of organization development. Are the outcomes relevant to the effectiveness of the client system? Is organization develop-

---

3   The boundaries of the client system which organization development affects may be a part (or subsystem) of the larger client system. For example, a client system like Aluminum Company of Canada has been directing the bulk of its organization development change program at one of its three main divisions. In the Esso change program, the refinery, a subsystem, became the chief client system. We will come back to this point later in our discussion of the strategy of implementation.

ment timely, economical, congruent with the anticipated client system trends, and so forth?

2. Is the cultural state of the client system ready for organization development?

What do we mean by "cultural readiness?" Each client system transmits and maintains a system of values that permeates the organization and is used as a basis for action and commitment. This does not mean that values are always adhered to, but it usually means that those who exemplify the values are rewarded and those who violate them are punished. Organization development also has a set of values. There is bound to be some conflict between these values and the values of the client system, but situations should be avoided where the two sets of value systems clash extraordinarily.

The degree and range of value conflicts provide some of the best clues for diagnosing the cultural state of the client system. That is, if the discrepancy between organization development values and the client system's values can be realistically assessed, a fairly good idea about the client system's readiness can be obtained. Let us sample some of the most important dimensions of the cultural state.

The *legitimacy of interpersonal relationships,* both in terms of its effects on the work and the degree to which members of the client system view it as susceptible to change, is an important aspect of the client system's culture. In many client systems, interpersonal phenomena are not considered appropriate to discuss, germane to the task, or legitimate as a focus of inquiry. As Henry Ford once said about his own philosophy of management: "All you have to do is to set the work before the men and they will do it." While this view is becoming slowly outdated by modern techniques of management, there are still many situations where interpersonal influence is regarded as invalid, illegitimate, or an invasion of privacy.

Another cultural variable which must be taken into account is the *control and authority system presently employed by the client system.* If it is too rigid and authoritarian, it may be too much at variance with the values of organization development.

The presence and intensity of conflict within the client system represents still another cultural factor which must be considered. It is difficult to generalize about conflict in terms of its relationship to the adoption of organization development. The impression we gain, however, is that it is best not to introduce organization development under conditions of intense conflict. In this case, the organization is under stress and may be *too* plastic; organization development may then be only a temporary dodge, become a tool in a power play, or be used later on as a convenient scapegoat. This is not to say that the type, causes, and intensity of conflict must be examined in relationship to the organization development program. (See volume in this series by Beckhard.)

The internal boundary system of the client system must be carefully examined in order to avoid situations where organization development values are internalized in one part of the system only to be rejected by and cause disruption in an adjacent part of the system.[4] In other words, the interdependence of the parts within the client system must be carefully scrutinized so that changes in some parts of the system do not backfire or create unanticipated negative repercussions in another part of the client system.

The last item to consider in assessing the cultural readiness of the client system is the most difficult to render in objective terms, and yet it is possibly the most important factor in estimating the probability of success. *It has to do with the change agent's relationship with the client system,* in particular, the quality and potentiality of the relationship.

If the change agent believes that it is possible to establish a relationship with the client system based on a healthy, realistic understanding of his role and with realistic expectations regarding the change, then a change program may be indicated. But if the relationship is based on fantasy, on unrealistic hopes, on fear or worship or intimidation, then the change agent and/or the client system must seriously re-examine the basis for their joint work.[5]

---

4   George Strauss and Alex Bavelas (1955) report an interesting example of this when a subunit of girls on an assembly line developed an ingenious new method which increased their job satisfaction and improved their performance significantly. The only trouble was that it had repercussions on interdependent parts of the organization. The program eventually had to be stopped. Though we know of no such case, it will be interesting to identify sources of strain that organization development might create with the client system's external boundary system: suppliers, customers, government, employee sources, etc. It is doubtful that it would generate the same degree of strain as internal interdependencies, but it still bears examination.

5   Let us be clear about this. We mean that if the change agent can foresee a healthy relationship in the future, he might well consider the organization development program. We do not think it is possible for the relationship to be totally trusting and realistic during the beginning phases of work. In any case, the main point we want to stress is the diagnostic validity of the relationship; the problems that inhere in that relationship are probably symptomatic of the problems to be encountered.

We are suggesting that one of the best ways of diagnosing cultural readiness has to do with the way the client system reacts to and establishes a relationship with the change agent. The quality and vicissitudes of this encounter—insofar as it is a miniature replica of the intended change program—provide an important clue regarding the fate of the organization development program.

What we mean by "readiness" is the degree of value conflict between organization development values and the client system's values in terms of: legitimacy of interpersonal phenomena; the range, depth, and intensity of conflicts and modes of conflict resolution; concepts of control and authority; the interdependence of parts of the client system; and the relationship between change agent and client system. Although they are difficult to measure precisely, thorough attention and rough assessment must be made before organization development can be introduced.

Assuming that the cultural readiness of the client system has been carefully assessed and found to be appropriate, we must ask:

3. Are the key people in the client system involved in or informed of the organization development program?

It can be disastrous if the people most affected by organization development are not involved, informed, or even advised of the program. To guarantee success, a great deal of energy and time must be devoted to assessing the extent to which the organization development program is supported by the key people and the attitudes individuals generally hold regarding organization development.

4. Are members of the client system adequately prepared and oriented to organization development?

The usual forms of preparation and orientation do not seem to be too effective for organization development, primarily because the word rarely conveys the sense of the experience. Organization development, if anything, is experience based, and words without an experimental referent often tend to confuse and, in some cases, cause more apprehension than necessary.

Some introductory *experiences* often prepare and orient future participants adequately. We have tried a miniature laboratory (waggishly called by one of the participants an "instant laboratory") to simulate as accurately as we could the laboratory environment. In this case, an entire laboratory was compressed into one full day of training. In other situations we have executed a specific training exercise with some prospective

TABLE 3-1.   Four-Step Model for Diagnosing State of Client System

1) Are organization development change goals appropriate to the target system?

   If not, stop and reconsider the appropriateness of organization development.

   If yes, then:

2) Is the cultural state of the client system prepared for organization development:
   a) Degree and type of value conflict?
   b) Legitimacy of interpersonal phenomena?
   c) Degree, range, intensity, resolution of conflict?
   d) Concepts of control, authority?
   e) Interdependence of client system?
   f) Relationship of trust and confidence between change agent and client system?

   If not, stop and examine areas where more preparation is needed or where value conflicts should be reduced.

   If yes, then:

3) Are key people involved and committed?

   If not, stop and examine ways of developing more commitment to program.

   If yes, then:

4) Are members of the client system adequately prepared and oriented to organization development?

   If not, stop and examine ways to develop more commitment to program.

delegates in order to give them a feel for the learning environment. In any case, we advocate some experience-based orientation in order to provide a reasonable facsimile of laboratory life.

The four-step model shown in Table 3-1 summarizes the above discussion.

Q.: What about the role of the "change agent," as you call it, or organization development consultant? What competencies should he have? How is he trained?

A.: I mentioned earlier that the idea of change agentry or organization development consultant is very new. Because of its novelty, its fundamental outline is still emerging. Thus, the role of the change agent is protean, changing, difficult to grasp, and practically impossible to generalize. However, it may be useful to make some tentative remarks about it.

The role of the change agent is *ambiguous.* Essentially, this means that the basic concept of the change agent is not widely understood and evokes a wide range of meaning. If one responds to the question, "What do you do?" with the answer, "I am a psychologist," it does not evoke the same bewilderment as the response, "I am a change agent." (In fact, the responder might be well advised not to answer in that vein.) The ambiguity of the role betrays its lack of legitimacy as well as credibility. It also involves certain risks such as drawing suspicion and hostility *because* of its ambiguity. On the other side, it can be helpful in providing the necessary latitude and breadth which more precisely defined roles do not allow.

The *competence* of the change agent must encompass a wide range of knowledge including:

1. conceptual diagnostic knowledge cutting across the entire sector of the behavioral sciences,

2. theories and methods of organizational change,

3. knowledge of sources of help, and

4. orientation to the ethical and evaluative functions of the change agent's role.

In addition to this intellectual grasp, the change agent must also possess the operational and relational skills of listening, observing, identifying, and reporting; ability to form relationships based on trust; and a high degree of behavioral flexibility. The change agent must be able also to use himself, to be in constant communication with himself, and to recognize and come to terms with (as much as humanly possible) his own motivations. Particularly in the diagnostic stages of the work the change agent must observe how the client system deals with him. Quite often, as mentioned earlier, the interface between the change agent and the client system is crucial for understanding and reaching a conclusion with respect to the state and readiness of the client system. In short, the change agent should be sensitive and mature.

Finally, the change agent should act congruently (authentically), in accordance with the values he is attempting to superimpose upon the client system's value system. The change agent must not impose democratic or humanistic values in an authoritarian or inhuman manner. If the change agent is concerned with creating more authenticity and collaboration, he must behave in ways that are in accord with these values. We say this not only for the obvious ethical reasons, but for deeper reasons as well. The fact of the matter is that so much of the change agent's influence grows out of his relationship with the client system and the extent to which he is emulated as a role model that any significant discrepancies between the change agent's actions and his stated values cannot help but create resistance.

These are the requirements for the effective achievement of the change agent's role. I would not expect to find many such supermen among us, but I would expect this job description to be used as an aim.

Q.: How do you define the client system? How do you decide with whom in the client system to consult? Just how and where do you decide to intervene?

A.: Your first question has to do with the crucial problem facing the organization development consultant: Who is the client? Is it the organization? Is it the group or person who appointed and pays the change agent? An individual in stress? This is a hard question to answer, and we would guess that the salient client shifts and oscillates among a host of different clients throughout the course of an organization development program. But the question itself should never be too far from the change agent's mind.

Where is the point of entry? That is, at what level of the organization should organization development be directed first? The top management group? Middle levels? Lower levels? There are some change agents, like Argyris (1962) and Blansfield (1962), who believe that change can succeed only if it starts at the top and percolates down; that in order for a real change to take place, the highest command must be the primary initiating force.

Others disagree with this strategy. They claim that change programs utilizing organization development can start at lower levels of the client system and still be successful. Furthermore, they argue, it is sometimes preferable to start the change at lower levels because in some situations, due to a variety of organizational conditions, starting at the top may be too risky.

Which systems are involved? Obviously everyone cannot be in the organization development program. This raises the question of priorities and choice. Can organization development be isolated in certain components of the organization, leaving other components without it? Or should attempts be made to include segments of all subsystems of the client system in the initial stages of the program? In any case, a careful diagnosis needs to be undertaken in order to trace the most strategic circulation of effects throughout the total client system. In my experience, some of the most critical unanticipated consequences arose when a diagnosis of the interdependencies of the subsystems within the client system was not carefully worked out.

How to choose the point of entry and which systems to involve are important and related strategic questions. There is no simple guideline to apply in making these choices, except an intimate knowledge and diagnosis of the client system which we outlined above, and a consideration of the model of change used.

Q.: To what extent can the change agent involve the client system in planning and executing organization development?

A.: In order to act in accordance with the values of organization development, the change agent should attempt to involve the client system in planning and goal setting for the change program. Sometimes this is easier said than done because the client system may not have the experience or expertise to collaborate realistically with the change agent. In any case, the change agent must attempt to make an adequate diagnosis of the extent to which the client system should be involved in the planning, goal setting, and execution of organization development.[6]

Q.: By the time you come to an agreement with the leaders of the organization, do you personally have a clear idea of your own goals? Do you have a specific change in mind, or just the general notion of being helpful, or of satisfying their need to achieve a particular result?

A.: Goals vary in clarity and kind and to make matters more confusing, they are always in the process of changing. When I feel certain that I know what *the* problem is, I begin to worry, and most of the time, for good

6   There is a dilemma here that is often commented upon by change agents and practitioners. How can systems of collaboration be established if one party to the encounter cannot adequately choose due to inexperience or lack of knowledge? Does coercion or faith have to be used during the very first phase of change?

reason. I usually try to develop with the client a set of "hoped for out-comes" which are measurable in terms of either productivity or human satisfaction, but these also shift a good deal as the evolution of the consultation progresses. Very often, I attempt to diagnose what the key problems of the client are in terms of the six basic areas of human concerns which I identified in Chapter 2, that is, whether or not any of the problems—integration, power and authority, collaboration, adaptation, identity, or revitalization—appear to be the most focal. For the most part, however, these six areas are all implicated in one way or another. The two chief changes I nearly always look for are these: First, is the organizational climate such that individuals are applying their energies and talents to the work with a sense of satisfaction and growth? Second, are people behaving and relating in such a way that the organizational climate approaches the conditions of a humane, just, and democratic society?

I have the general conviction that in 90% of the organization development cases I have worked on, the organization *itself* can unblock and facilitate real progress toward its goals if it will expend the energy to find out what its blocks and frustrations are. Only rarely do I find that new personnel or technology imported from the outside is required. In other words, the organization development consultant, like the therapist, tries to identify those factors which impede the development, rather than tinker with the system like a mechanic repairing a broken machine or like a technician who wants to add or replace a part. So that this point will not be misunderstood, I should say that there *are* cases where new skills and technologies are required but, for the most part, organization development relies heavily on identifying and facilitating the talent that exists.

Q: How do you decide when to stop your consultation? How do you terminate? How do you evaluate your contribution to the organization?

A.:   This is a tough question to answer, as you know, for evaluations of "progress" and "health" are difficult at best. Some organization development practitioners, such as Blake and Mouton (in this series) attempt to use "hard" productivity figures, whether they be numbers produced or cost factors or waste, etc. Others use a variety of indicators based on "people" factors, such as satisfaction, communication patterns, morale, etc. Still others tend to focus on whether the social system itself is approaching some or most of the goals outlined in response to your first question. Even if such measures are available to me, and often they are not, I try to ascertain if the organization now contains the resources of people and competence to maintain and continue its own organization development program.

I think I could clarify this point by showing you a letter I wrote to the "training committee" of XYZ Corporation, a firm I consulted for for about five years or so. After five years, most of the top executives, indeed all of the managerial force down to the foremen, had a strong commitment toward and exposure to organization development activities. The "training committee" itself was a product of the organization development program and consisted of the President, Vice President of Personnel, Vice President of Production, and virtually the entire top management group.

TO: XYZ TRAINING COMMITTEE
FROM: Warren G. Bennis
SUBJECT: Organization Development

In the five years or so that I have been associated with XYZ, as friend and consultant, I have kept true to an old maxim: "If you're interested in change, don't write memos." I depart from this wisdom now only to set forth a few thoughts on the future, which always meets us sooner than we expected.

It seems to me that XYZ is now in a position where it should consciously decide or decide consciously *not to decide* on future directions in organization development. I recommend that the following steps be taken:

1. A deliberate, conscious strategy should be developed (maybe even in the form of a "white paper") which would articulate the goals, strategies, and time perspective of XYZ's organization development. Included in this statement should be an understanding of the "total system," which means an analysis of interdependencies and lack of it among and between various XYZ subsystems. Included in this also should be the relationship between residential "cousins," labs, family groups, the use of external consultants, etc.

2. There should be more and more attention to strengthening internal XYZ change resources, rather than uneven reliance on external consultants. (I am talking about balance here. I am not recommending, necessarily, a decrease in external consultants. I am recommending the development of internal change agents and internal strength and skills for change.)

I think this could be accomplished in the following ways:

a. A development of an organization development program or department to coordinate all the activities under this general heading.

b. An advisory committee, essentially the same membership of the Training Committee plus a few training consultants, to serve as a policy-making adjunct to the organization development program.

c. A more concerted effort to develop research as part of the consulting-training effort.

3. More direct linkages between XYZ clients and external consultants working as a "project team" on problems. This has already begun and should be encouraged. The NTL associated universities in the Industrial Consortium should be tapped as possible sources of team membership (e.g., UCLA, Case, M.I.T., Harvard, Michigan, etc.). The important thing here is that the organization development program should serve as the marriage broker, putting external consultants and internal change agents together and taking responsibility to help them become a team, commonly devoted to solving problems as they appear and with flexible deployment.

4. Development of an XYZ organization development interne program. This could be accomplished by setting up specially tailored XYZ programs or by sending qualified people to change agent programs.

I write this recommendation with a spirit of great satisfaction with XYZ and their progress. I do think we're ready to turn a corner and to become more deliberate and programmatic in the decade ahead.

In writing this letter, my intentions were to see whether the training committee could take stock and consider anew what directions they wanted to go in with respect to organization development. In addition, I wanted to see whether they could wean themselves from outside consultants and start developing their own resources from internal candidates. I thought that if XYZ Corporation could achieve these goals in a reasonable period of time, I would feel easier about terminating with the knowledge that they now "owned" the resources so necessary to continue the organization development effort. So the task I set before them was for me the "test" of whether or not the XYZ Corporation could work on its own. This test, from my own point of view, along with other indicators of goal attainment, provides at least two ways for making what almost always turns out to be a very difficult determination.

These are some of the main questions which perplex change agents in initiating change programs. They do not exhaust the endless possibilities of problems. And until we have achieved perfect strategic comprehension of the client system in relationship to the change agent, we will be beset by these and still other unanticipated problems.

The four-step model and the other considerations reviewed above provide a rough view of the conditions that I would find applicable to your questions. Though, I must add, that one never finds the "perfect" client system any more than one finds the "perfect" student or "perfect" patient. Moreover, there are other more personal feelings and convictions that enter into account when deciding about a client. One was hinted at earlier; namely, that one doesn't have the time to do all one wants. This is true for the researcher, consultant, or, for that matter, any professional. More subtle than "role overload" is the difficult to articulate, but nonetheless very real, *affinities* that one feels for certain individuals within the client system. Though I have never seen it discussed in the literature on organization development, I am positive that human compatibility and affection play a very large role both in the decision to participate in an organization development change effort and in the ultimate success of the program. Finally, I should add that the organization itself, its values, goals, and product, play a major role in whether or not I will engage in an organization development relationship. Some of my colleagues, for example, refuse to participate in any organization development program connected with the "military complex." During recent years, particularly the last two years, since assuming an academic administrative role, I have worked, where time permits, only with universities.

Unlike the older professions, where the focus is on disease or delinquency or sin, organization development is a practice that involves a normative stance, that is, it is a program that concentrates on health and improvement, not simply on cure. To the extent that this is true, all change agents make moral choices—whether they like it or not—when they decide to participate (or not) in an organization development program.

4

QUESTIONS AND ANSWERS: ORGANIZATION DEVELOPMENT

PART II: THE PRACTITIONERS

The preceding chapter covers a number of questions that were generated by a group of psychiatrists interested in organization development. What might be useful now is a set of questions applicable to another group, the practitioners, that is, potential consumers of organization development. This opportunity presented itself two years ago at the annual meeting of the National Association of Manufacturers where an entire morning of the proceedings was devoted to organization development. After the panelists finished their own talks, the audience raised a number of questions about the practical aspects of organization development. The talks and questions and answers were later published in a National Association of Manufacturers' publication entitled, *What's Wrong with Work?* (1967). What follows is an elaboration of the responses I made to questions asked at that meeting.

Q.: Where might an organization development program start in an organization?

A.: Organization development programs can start in a variety of ways and at a variety of levels. Some organization development consultants believe that programs can start at any level. And Richard Beckhard reports (*What's Wrong with Work?*, 1967, p. 50) that he has found that the most effective programs have often started low down in the organization with only partial commitment from the top. Later, after the evidence of the effect was in, the top came to be fully committed. I stated in the last chapter that organization development programs can begin anywhere so long as there is some kind of "umbrella" protection from the next highest echelon and so long as the other systems that relate to the client are aware of, if not committed to, the goals of the organization development program.

So there are many ways to start. Some people get excited intellectually, and begin reading some of the recent behavioral science and management literature. Some people go to a T-group and find a new way of viewing managerial realities, a new way of looking at life. Other people learn through osmosis, or through examples, or they might even learn by attending a meeting—like this one. A company president I know said his firm started an organization development program after his wife went through a T-group.

Q.: Who might start an organization development program?

A.: One interesting thing I've noticed is that within almost all organizations there is a group of people who get labeled chronic complainers. Actually, they are often people who are very sensitive to the discrepancy between what *is possible* and what *is*. They are the "problem finders," or what Douglas Bunker refers to as "variance sensors."

These individuals who sense variance between what *is* and what *is possible* quite often make a very good cadre, or a good beginning team for organization development. Some organization development consultants attempt very early in their experience to identify these "variance sensors" and bring them together in a "critical mass" as a way of starting the organization development effort. Historically, it is interesting to note that many of our creative revolutions and important breakthroughs have started in just this way: people who want a new order, a new form. Lo and behold, once they start articulating their goals, even with a small following, others join in.

If one opens his ears to these people, whether we call them "variance sensors" or agents of change, maybe they can make a beginning if you can get them to start talking to one another.

Basically, I prefer John Paul Jones' response to the question "Where is the best place to start an organization development program?" the best. He said: "With you. Everybody wants to start with the other guy." (*What's Wrong with Work?*, 1967, p. 50)

Q.: Are organization development concepts applicable in times of decreasing sales and increasing costs?

A.: More so. The question implies that organization development is a luxury that can be tried when there is enough slack in the system. The whole point that I am trying to make is that it isn't just *nice* to have organization development, it's *necessary*. Given the changes taking place in society and the turbulence and uncertainty of the environment I tried to sketch out in Chapter 2, unless management keeps its eye on organization development, it's not going to be able to manage the future. It's not a matter of one's ethics or values or being a nice guy. It's a question of how we develop the best form of organization to be able to cope with a very difficult and changing environment. Organization development is simply one mechanism by which the organization can understand and then cope with this problem.

Q.: How do you use organization development concepts to induce people to join an organization, particularly at the lower levels? And how do students feel about organization development?

A.: We've heard a lot in recent years about students—particularly the brighter ones—turning their backs on business as a career. I think it's clear that the younger generation is not attracted to conformity; it's not attracted to interests narrowly defined around profit concerns or to being enmeshed in a hierarchical system with limited responsibility. As a matter of fact, if there is one distinguishing characteristic of the student activists as well as many other young professionals, it is their *anti-hierarchical* values.

In contrast, organization development concepts encourage people to develop their potentialities within the organizational framework and emphasize individual responsibility and problem-solving. These are all much more congruent with the younger generation's needs and goals. I think any company with a strong organization development program is missing the boat in its recruiting effort if it fails to publicize its organization development approach to managing. This would be a real plus to many young people in making a decision about a job.

Q.: How do you answer the cry of busy executives who say they can't make the extra investment in time that organization development seems to require?

A.: It depends primarily on their seeing the true significance of organization development for the growth (and survival!) of the organization. If they regard organization development as some rather esoteric training philosophy, somewhat like, for example, the Aspen Conferences on the Great Books, then they have clearly missed the point of the functional necessity for organization development. (I would also suggest that these "busy executives" take a look at Chapter 2 of this volume for an elaboration of the "busy environment.")

Q.: You have discussed "temporary systems" and a non-hierarchical structure consisting of task forces which can be deployed as a new model of organizations to replace the traditional hierarchical form. In this new form of organization, composed of these temporary systems, what will constitute the home base for the worker? Where will he return?

A.: Of course there will have to be some form of organizational structure, although, as I said in Chapter 2, it will differ substantially from our present forms. And there will be hierarchies, too, though based on other than such mechanical factors as status. Hierarchy will be a function of competence, closeness to the relevant information and action, and other criteria that are germane to the actual solving of problems.

Such systems are being used in more and more organizations today, which only means that people come together for a short period of time to solve a problem or complete a project rather than operating as a permanent team or group. As a matter of fact, there are some interesting data which indicate that the younger the team is, the more effective and innovative it is; the older the team, the more stodgy and less innovative. I refer to the age of the team, the length of time the members have been working together, not the average age of the team members.

As far as the "home base" goes, this can take different forms. Actually, the temporary system itself and consecutive ones can provide an effective home base. I am not at all sure that static, unchanging groups provide the home base referred to, in any case. A man's work, his commitment to a career, and his identification with the adaptive process, it seems to me, can provide the necessary ingredients for his continuity in a changing world.

Q.: Along these lines, will the mobile executive you describe, moving from one group to the next, exchanging roles and status almost as often as he buys a new car, feel the kind of commitment and constancy of drive that has been required for the success of a company in the past?

A.: He'll have the drive all right. But the commitment will be more qualified, more directed to the processes of problem-solving than to the specific content of the job. He will be more committed to a *career* and continual learning than the *job*. Before Robert McNamara was appointed to the top Defense post, he was also considered for the Treasury and State departments. It was felt that he could manage any of these well because he is a "problem-solver." In contrast, the colonel in the movie "The Bridge on the River Kwai" was so obsessed by ritual, with doing the job the way he'd always done it, that under totally different conditions, which called for a new response, he continued the old pattern. Managers of the future will be committed to problem-solving, to contingency and change.

This takes both emotional stability and courage, but it is difficult for me to see how men can respond adaptively to change unless they know who they are and can gain intrinsic satisfaction from solving problems, whether the problem is in the area of marketing, student unrest, cities, transportation, production, or you name it. The specific target of the problem will change, but the need to direct and harness problem-solving capacities will continue to press upon us.

As I've suggested, more and more of us will have to develop portable roots, whether it's the family, some professional calling, or fidelity, as a solid "home base." John Cage wrote a little triplet which puts it so well:

We carry our homes
within us
which enables us to *fly*.

5

THE PROBLEM OF "SENSITIVITY TRAINING"

Throughout this volume and others in this series, mention is made frequently of the uses of "sensitivity training" for organization development. Sensitivity training is a novel and controversial form of education which goes under a variety of names: laboratory training or education (which I prefer and will employ for convenience here), Encounter Groups, "T" Groups, "L" (for learning) Groups, Self-analytic Groups, and many more. Essentially, laboratory training is a small group effort designed to make its participants more aware of themselves and of the group process. The group works under the guidance of a professionally competent behavioral scientist and explores group processes and development through focusing attention on the experienced behavior of its members. The group itself is relatively unstructured and finds its own way, so to speak, by coming together to understand itself.

Any educational experience that is as novel as laboratory training and that precipitates as much curiosity (and anxiety) is bound to become controversial. Laboratory training certainly has become at once more controversial *and* popular. It gains fierce advocates (called "cultists" by the other side) and equally devout detractors. Obviously, any educational device that can arouse so much controversy deserves serious examination and research. Research *is* being conducted at many universities (though far from enough), for example, at M.I.T., State University of New York at Buffalo, Harvard Business School, and Boston University, to name a few. However, I suspect that, regardless of how much research is conducted, laboratory training will always be a controversial issue, because it raises questions about the very nature of man, his attitudes, feelings, and sense of well-being. Most formal educational strategies focus exclusively on man as a rational-cognitive being. That's what we come to expect of education, particularly higher and adult education. Laboratory training, on the other hand, takes man's emotional life as its central issue and seeks to determine how these emotions affect his relationships with others and his capacity for attaining high competence. It focuses on life experiences that ordinarily are bypassed or ignored, man's affective regions. So in a society where work and love are regarded as mutually exclusive (and where a man having—or worse, expressing—"feelings" is regarded as "effeminate"), where education is a reserved domain for the intellect only, where "classroom experiences" are typically highly structured, goal-directed, and authoritarian, it should come as no surprise that laboratory training is and will continue to be "controversial."

What complicates matters, of course, is that there are individual differences and different styles of learning. Some people take immediately to the "unstructuredness" and to the initially chaotic situation of the laboratory learning experience. Others find it unrewarding and "a waste of time." I suspect that highly defensive people and people who are not particularly "open" to new experiences might also encounter, certainly at first, more anxiety than they find tolerable. Laboratory training, compared to, say, therapy groups, presupposes a higher degree of emotional health. In other words, unlike group therapy, laboratory training is an educational program designed to enhance life, not to cure emotional problems.

More significant for me than individual styles of learning and defensiveness, however, is the organizational context within which laboratory training is used. In Chapter 3, I discussed in some detail the environmental conditions which lead to successful organization development outcomes. It might be useful, at this point, to examine those conditions which lead to failure. To dramatize this, I will present three cases in which laboratory training (in one form or another) failed. From these cases, we can derive some general propositions about situations for which the technique is appropriate and those for which it is unsuitable.

THREE CASES OF FAILURE [1]

In medical training, students and physicians are exposed quite regularly to an intriguing ordeal called the Clinical Pathology Conference in which a

1   Adapted from Schein and Bennis (1965). Reprinted by permission of the publisher, John Wiley & Sons, Inc. (New York).

pathologist presents the autopsy of a patient and some expert is called in (in full view of all seated in the amphitheater) to diagnose the precise cause of the fatality. No equivalent teaching device exists in the behavioral sciences, mainly because we are in a relatively early state of developing a practice.[2] Yet we thought it might be interesting to present several examples of failure or partial failure in order to dramatize and clarify different parts of this chapter. We hope these examples will help in formulating some principles which we propose in the next section.

What we propose to do is this: We will present three brief anecdotes or actual cases that have come to our attention in one way or another. (We have doctored and disguised the cases sufficiently so that no confidences will be endangered). The cases will be presented consecutively and without comment until the third and last one; then we will attempt to develop some principles from the case material.

Case 1: A Letter from a Government Training Center

This is a letter which came to one of the authors from a government training officer (Dr. A) connected with a large government training center. Laboratory training was started at the center several months before and since that time the following things happened: (1) the Director (Mr. Z) went to a two-week laboratory at Bethel, (2) about 250 government officials underwent a five-day laboratory at the center under Dr. A's leadership with other staff drawn from officials Dr. A had personally trained, and (3) Dr. A with the support of Mr. B (a strong advocate of laboratory training and second in command of the center) planned to set up a laboratory training experience for all 2,000 officials stationed there. This letter arrived shortly after plans were laid out to train trainers in order to execute a massive design.

. . . I'm still behind on the reports on our lab training here, at least on the reports I'd like to get out.

Some of the little things that have cropped up. The Director who went to the two-week lab away from here feels that those who have only gone through four or five days training here don't really have the capacity to talk to him.

Those members of the faculty who got the training late wonder why they were left to last. An "in" group and "out" group developed in the

2　There are other reasons as well: for example, the understandable secrecy regarding failures or mixed successes and the difficulty in attributing precise causality in these complex social change ventures.

faculty. Some of the outs resented being trained by one of their peers. Some wanted to know: "How did you get to be a trainer?"

The head of our medical department told the Director that lab training type of training is dangerous.

The chief in Washington (over our Director!) asked someone in an aside: "What the hell is Dr. A doing giving that kind of training!"

A Grade 15 called in a Grade 12 scheduled to attend a five-day lab in April and said, not once but twice: "You don't have to go to this thing you know. I want you to understand it is entirely voluntary, you don't have to go unless you want to... What are you going to do if some younger official tells you he doesn't like the way you conduct yourself?"

One man comes up to me occasionally, looks around as if to make sure no one is watching, and then makes the sign of T with both hands.

The Director's deputy wrote a letter to Headquarters and asked for an evaluation of lab training. "If it's good for one, is it good for all?"

I received an informal request from a staff official in Headquarters asking me to answer about 12 objections commonly raised to lab training.

In short, a considerable number of anxieties have been raised. Some are intrigued, some are scared.

Two weeks elapsed and another letter arrived from Dr. A:

... We have unfortunately hit a snag. How serious it will be remains to be seen. Mr. B (Dr. A's main line support) has been transferred. This removed our chief advocate suddenly. Within a week the Director, Mr. Z, called in the Head of Curriculum and outlined how he wanted lab training put into the curriculum. A meeting was set up with me, the Director, and the Head of Curriculum.

(Up until this time we had been planning, with Mr. B's approval and backing, to put the training into one department and start in September. We proposed, if we could get the money, to get two outside trainers in for three weeks in August, to train this Department's staff. Someone from National Training Laboratories had been down and talked this over with the staff and I had managed to find a friend in Washington who said he would underwrite the program. We had not gotten down to the nuts and bolts of actually drawing up detailed plans for September, but that was the large outline.)

In the May 3rd meeting, Mr. Z started out by saying NTL didn't have any final answers to lab training and that his trainers at Arden House were quick to admit they didn't know all the answers. Thus, he said, we had a chance to strike out on our own and did not have to be bound by the fixed two-weeks approach pioneered by NTL. (Up to this time he was the only one who had been insisting on two weeks; we had been talking in terms of four and five days). Furthermore, we could not have officials foregoing their vacations in August, so any ideas about giving them three weeks of training couldn't be considered. Anyway, it didn't take much training because all his trainers did was sit there, they hardly opened their mouths during the two weeks. He would train the officials himself and he thought possibly one afternoon would be enough. What he proposed then was that after about six or seven weeks all the students be given one or two days to give each other feedback. This would be preceded by four or five lectures during the first week or so which would tell them what to be watching for. Keeping what they had observed in mind, they could then tell each other after the sixth week what they had observed. At the end of school, the students would be given another day or two days to give each other feedback. And so on. One or two of us tried to offer some comments or observations and were either cut off or ignored. As a consultant of sorts, I didn't feel quite up to exploring all the implications of his plan in front of the staff because I felt it was his prerogative to run the school as he wanted to.

Since that time various staff sections have been busy trying to pass on to other staff sections the job of trying to figure out what Mr. Z wants and making plans for his wishes. I've been invited to a meeting in the morning and will see what develops. I intend to talk to Mr. Z by himself after this if I can.

I'm curious to find out if he will tell me why he changed his mind, apparently, so suddenly and why he chose not to build on any of the data we had so painstakingly gathered. All this he just threw out of the window. And either just before or just after the May 3rd meeting he forwarded to Headquarters a report of the school activities in which he asked for funds for the August training I described.

We are unable to figure out whether Mr. B's leaving triggered the change, whether he is scared to try a four-day lab with students, whether he balks at paying the training price, whether he is irked at me, or just what the score is. But what makes it so hard to figure is that all the reports, letters, plans, etc., that he has seen and signed have nothing to do with what he has proposed. Some of what he says might be worked out into something quite useful, but in the meeting he brooked no comment— all he wanted was a rubber stamp.

I am not ready at this point to say the effort has failed because a lot of pressure has been building up in the past ten days. How much it will mean has yet to be disclosed. Certainly, at this moment the plans for the

August training seem dead, although we may yet get the test in one Department rather than among 800 students. This really bugged me, trying something completely unknown and untested on 800 men.

Several weeks following this letter, Dr. A called to say that the Government Training Center had stopped its laboratory training and "had gone back to more traditional training methods."

Case 2: A Letter from Medical Services

This letter was sent as a confidential memorandum from the chief medical officer of a large manufacturing company to the Vice President of Personnel. A copy of this memo was sent to Dr. A, chief training officer for the company. Dr. A had been hiring consultants who use laboratory training quite regularly in their work for this company.

The medical division is concerned about the possibility of medical casualties from the T-group type of training program.

Dr. Jones says that T-group programs have greater likelihood of producing a higher percentage of disabling mental disturbances than do ordinary work situations.

The purpose of the Training Division is training.

The purpose of Medical Division is the prevention of illness and disability.

We feel the purpose of our Division warrants our scrutiny of any Company activity likely to be related to disabilities.

We recommended several months ago that the list of candidates for training sessions be passed before the local Company medical officer for his approval or comment regarding the names thereon. The suggestion is held impractical by some on the basis that the Company medical officers are not psychologically or psychiatrically oriented, have little knowledge or comprehension concerning the nature of the sessions, and are not qualified to determine who are high-risk candidates. It is my conviction that something along the following lines should be required by the Company, if for no other reason than the doubt surrounding the advisability of having therapy for medical conditions unsupervised by medical people:

a)   Collaboration should start immediately to arrange a long weekend session in a suitable place, to be attended by the senior medical representative from each of our plants. Dr. A should prepare a clear statement of the purpose of these T-sessions, a clear statement of the procedure used in attempting to achieve the purpose, a clear statement on what these procedures demand from the individual, and a clear statement of the signs which the trainers use as indicators of impending disability, no matter how temporary. In addition, this working session should provide a sample experience for the doctors attending. The purpose of this session would be to take away any feeling that the local doctor was completely "clueless" regarding what is appearing to take on the shadowy form of a mystic cult; . . .

This case had a reasonably successful outcome. The chief medical officer himself attended a two-week laboratory at Bethel and shortly after his return organized a long weekend session that was led by two laboratory trainers, for all of his doctors, other key personnel and line officials. This 3-day weekend session was designed as a modified laboratory, and, according to the participants and the trainers, it accomplished its purposes: a better understanding of laboratory training by the doctors, and an improvement in the collaboration between medical and training divisions.

Case 3: The Undercover Change Agent

The following anecdote is based on interviews conducted with members of an organization in which laboratory training was tried and failed. The training endeavor was almost totally disastrous: the staff member conducting the laboratory training was fired, his colleague transferred; the director of training was ordered to stop all training connected with management development and to provide only technical training; the Vice President of Personnel resigned.

The company itself is a large retailing combine operating about fifteen department stores in the Midwest. The headquarters are located in Milwaukee and many of the branch stores are located in the conservative, German farming centers throughout Wisconsin and Minnesota. The company is family-owned and operated by the son of the founder, Mr. Hess.

The company committed itself to a considerable amount of executive training through its personnel department. Each year most of its managerial staff attended a one-week course at a small hotel in the lake country near Milwaukee. For the most part, the human relations training was based on cases very like those collected and used at the Harvard Business School. These case courses were deemed very successful by management and by the participants.

Last year the company hired a new trainer (Mr. Jones) for their one-week human relations training program. Before taking the job, Jones attended a two-week laboratory and was deeply impressed by the experience. After several weeks of conducting case-study discussions, Jones asked his boss, the director of training, if they could try some laboratory training. The director of training did not understand it completely but said he would take the matter up with his boss, the Vice President of Personnel. The latter had only an inkling of what laboratory training was all about but passed on whatever he knew to the President. It was not at all clear who "cleared what with whom" or how much anyone understood about the idea of laboratory training, but, in any case, nine weeks of laboratory training took place with nine different groups, all at the lower echelons of management. During the ninth week the President arrived unannounced at the training site and demanded to be given entry into the T-groups. Jones refused at first but finally gave in to the President's orders.

Shortly after the President's return to Milwaukee, the training ceased and Jones was fired, etc. What had happened?

Leading up to the President's visit to the laboratory, which culminated in his storming into the resort hotel during the breakfast hour demanding entrance into the T-group, was a whole series of events. First of all, the President had heard about some "interesting" training going on, quite unlike what he had come to expect from case-study discussions. He knew nothing about this "group dynamics business" and was angry at not being told about it. Second, rumors had come to his attention that some "hanky panky" was going on there. In fact, the Vice President of Buying had overheard a conversation between two of his assistant buyers that was reported to the President. One of the buyers had just returned from a one-week laboratory and the other buyer was quizzing her about it. The conversation the Vice President reported to the President went something like this:

Buyer A: Oh, you just came back from Marlboro? (the training site)
Buyer B: Yes.
Buyer A: How was it?
Buyer B: This course was the deepest experience I have had in my life so far . . . Can you imagine, there was one man who took off his clothes completely!
Buyer A: A striptease?
Buyer B: Uh huh.

Apparently, Buyer B was attempting to indicate to A the depth of the experience, the emotional revelations. In fact, what Buyer A passed on to her boss was that a literal striptease took place at Marlboro. To this day there are some places in the company where this story is still believed.

There had been an attempted suicide by one of the participants in the training shortly after his return from the week at Marlboro.

Finally, whenever the President asked his Vice President of Personnel whether he visited Marlboro and whether he was aware of what was going on there, the Vice President said he did not really know what was going on and that he was advised by Mr. Jones to stay away. These events led to the President's surprise visit to Marlboro.

He arrived at Marlboro at breakfast in the third day of a week's program and demanded his entrance in the T-group. According to Jones:

I tried to dissuade him but to no avail. He insisted that he had the right. "If you have nothing to hide," he said, "then let me in. If you have something to hide, then I must find out." So he observed us for a two hour T-session. After the meeting I told him that it was hard to get a realistic picture of what goes on in T-groups. He noted this and smiled at my remarks and expressed astonishment about the lack of structure in the group.

After the meeting, while having coffee, he voiced a little surprise about my passive attitude and my not exercising leadership at all. I tried to explain to him how important this is, but I felt there was an enormous wall of prejudice I could not get behind.

Then I gave a lecture to the group on leadership, drawing most of my material from McGregor's *The Human Side of Enterprise.* Then I asked the participants to organize the last day's training activities. . .

In the afternoon, right after their second T-group of the day, when people were on their feet, the President rose and told everyone to remain in their seats and then delivered a twenty-minute speech. He first said that supervisory training was an important thing and that the company had already spent a lot of money on it. He thought the participants were getting something from the company which was not at all self-evident that a company would do for its people. Then he went on to say that these are critical times, that the competitive situation was worsening, and that success would require the greatest effort of everybody. This could be achieved, he said, by working hard and by following the given orders without question—all the requisites, I thought, of a paternalistic management. He went on speaking then like a military leader. Then he referred to my short lecture on leadership and said that there was one point he did not agree with at all. (One of the participants asked if a subordinate always has to follow orders to the word. I gave a very qualified answer trying to show that there could be conditions for questioning a superior.) The President said that he most strongly wanted to emphasize that a subordinate had better follow orders—there was no question about that! Then he went into a monologue about leadership philosophy all of which ended up as a flat contradiction of the whole philosophy of the course. People were baffled by this sudden outbreak by the President and there was a certain amount of confusion about it. The participants realized that here were two exponents of two different philosophies. . . .

Here is the President's version of that fateful day!

They were discussing group relations, I guess. They were sitting in a circle and they would sit silent for awhile and they would ask: "What is your impression of me and what do others make of me? And I'd like to tell you what I think of you, Jane, or you, Jim." Then there would be silence, long silence and the pressure and tension would steadily mount and then it would explode and everyone would start talking at once about impressions people had of each other. They would "give feedback," they said. I don't know, I suppose that one can learn a lot about how one feels and sees, but I did not think that this kind of discussion was crucial for management training. Matter of fact, some of it seemed like communism to me; they've gone too far for me, too revolutionary!

PROPOSITIONS ABOUT THE USES OF
LABORATORY TRAINING IN EFFECTING SOCIAL CHANGE

We have attempted to present the risks and promises of engineering social change in target systems via laboratory training. The three cases of failure, because of their dramatic aspects, should not blind us to the fact that these are the exception, not the rule. On the other hand, abnormal as these three cases may be, it would be a mistake to regard them only for their pathological interest. What we would like to do now is consider both the successes and the failures and develop propositions about social change which are related to and clearly build upon the second section of this chapter concerning the considerations for the successful adoption of laboratory training by social systems.[3]

3   These principles can encompass any planned social change, not only those directed by laboratory training.

- *In undertaking any planned social change using laboratory training, the core of the target system values must not be too discrepant with the laboratory training values.*

Every target system has a core of values that characterizes it and determines a good deal of its decisions. Laboratory training, also, has a system of core values. We discussed these earlier in terms of legitimacy of interpersonal phenomena, concepts of control, and so forth. We stated then that the target system's values should be somewhat in accord with, or *potentially* congruent to, laboratory training values. Where the two systems of values are widely discrepant and rigid, and where the value system of the target cannot yield without vitally endangering the target system's core values, change induced by laboratory training will probably not succeed.

Let us be specific. In the case of the Government Training Center and the department store, it is obvious that the institutional base was perceived, by men in power, as seriously threatened. The values, the normative patterns, the set of shared expectations were all in flux due to the training endeavors of Dr. A and Mr. Jones.

Perhaps the central issue here concerns the definition of the word "training." *Webster's Dictionary* defines it as follows: "(1) To subject oneself or be subjected to instruction, drilling, regular exercise, dieting, etc. (2) To form habits or impart proficiency [by] teaching, drilling, etc." Most training affirms these definitions; training is a process whereby individuals learn the skills, attitudes, and orientation congruent to a particular role. Training, viewed this way, has a conservative connotation. It takes organizations as they are and attempts to shape individuals to them.

What we have been calling training is probably misnamed. For certainly a program that aims to change the very structure of the organization through modifying a role orientation is not training in the usual sense of this word. This is not only a semantic issue. Training, in its dictionary sense and in the way that most personnel managers use it and top management construes it, is viewed conservatively: fitting people to roles. Training in the sense that it was employed in these cases signifies a *fundamental* change, an alteration of the values, norms, and patterns of expectations. In this sense President Hess was completely correct in viewing laboratory training as "revolutionary" and Mr. Z was perfectly justified in going slowly on laboratory training at the military base. It is revolutionary insofar as the core of institutional values which leadership was striving to preserve was basically threatened by the laboratory training change programs.

Putting it a bit differently, most organizations agree to various training and development programs insofar as they strengthen the core of institutional values and insofar as they facilitate the functioning of the organization. When programs are seen as imperiling the institutional base, we can expect the strong resistance evinced in these cases.

But most social change programs, certainly laboratory training, attempt to alter institutional values. How, then, can the inevitable and powerful resistance be reduced?

- *In undertaking any planned social change, legitimacy for the change must be gained through obtaining the support of the key people.*

This is not to say that laboratory training should start at the top; it does mean that a careful and deliberate effort must be made to gain acceptance by the top management group. Without this, the laboratory training is constantly in peril. Notice what happened when Mr. B (the top line official in the government center supporting laboratory training) was transferred: the program came apart at the seams. If Mr. B's successor had been well briefed and oriented, and if Mr. Z were briefed and oriented, then the program might have had more resilience to shock. The same is true regarding the department store case: Nobody really seemed to know "what was up" except possibly Jones. And if the Vice President of Personnel had been able and competent to tell President Hess what was really going on at Marlboro, then it might not have been necessary for him to make the surprise trip.

In any case, efforts must be made to provide top management with as clear and realistic a picture of laboratory training as possible. This is done not only as an acquaintance process but also as a test of top management's commitment toward the potential changes. If the commitment is weak at the top level, then a total re-evaluation of the strategy is required. It is far better to discover this early than late. In the case of the department store, partly out of fear and mostly from futility, the training staff worked surreptitiously, with the faint hope that the training effects would be accepted. The outcome produced an unstable situation where the lowest levels of management maintained values that were in conflict with top management. The tension created by this value conflict was reduced by removing its source, Jones, and restoring the old orientation.

Obtaining hierarchical acceptance, no matter how painstaking and difficult, provides at least some guarantee that management can understand, and hence, manage the change without undue tension.

· *In undertaking any planned social change, the process of installing the change programs must be congruent with the process and goals of such programs.*

We are talking here of a fairly simple, but crucial, matter. The change agent should know what he is doing and should act congruently and authentically. While we are not absolutely confident of this proposition holding in every situation (installing a totalitarian system, for example), we are sure that this is essential for a democratic change program. For reasons that appeared sensible at the time, Jones operated more as an undercover agent than as an agent of change. It is doubtful that he understood the consequences of his decisions: The fact that he viewed laboratory training as a simple substitute for the case method gives rise to this question. Were the goals and *meta-goals* of laboratory training clearly understood by the change agents?

It is not obvious that they were understood. Jones, in particular, violated to some degree the meta-goals: authenticity was abandoned by the underground methods used to start the program. Action was taken without a spirit of inquiry, and the nature of the change program was far from a collaborative one. The way Dr. A dealt with Mr. Z and the way Mr. Jones dealt with President Hess were not examples of authentic and collaborative relationships.

Unanticipated consequences can jeopardize any change program. Only the omniscient can be blamed for those. But in the case of the department store, many of the consequences could have been foreseen and avoided—if Jones had used the processes of laboratory training in installing the change program. What we observed instead was the blind use of a tool in a way which contradicted its essence.

· *In undertaking any planned social change, the employment security of the change agent must be guaranteed.*

Blau (1961) points out that one of the prerequisites for adaptation in bureaucracy is the minimum employment security of the personnel. In terms of the brute reality of existence this means that most people would not risk their jobs in order to create change. Given the laboratory training approach to organizational change, minimum employment security is essential for the change agent, particularly if he is a member of the organization. The training staff must maintain their separateness from other company employees and must develop some discretion and autonomy insofar as training functions are concerned.

For Jones there was no real alternative but to let the President sit in; it was either that or dismissal. If a situation similar to that one occurred but the trainer had maximum employment security or was an outside consultant, employed temporarily by the company, possibly there would have been a different outcome.

- *In undertaking any planned social change utilizing laboratory training, the voluntary commitment of the participants may be a crucial factor in the success of the program.*

We have discussed this at some length earlier. But for emphasis we repeat that the difficulty of describing laboratory training through verbal orientation, plus the problematic aspects of organizational legitimacy to influence interpersonal behavior, lead to only one conclusion with respect to participant attendance at laboratories. This is that all delegates must undertake laboratory training in a completely voluntary spirit. It is highly doubtful that they will learn if this condition does not prevail.

- *In undertaking any planned social change utilizing laboratory training, the legitimacy of interpersonal influence must be potentially acceptable.*

The spread and belief of the "striptease" rumor shows the desirability of an orientation for prospective participants. But it shows more than that. We must ask: How much and in what way can (should) an organization influence the personalities of its employees? It is not exactly obvious that interpersonal competence is correlated with effective role functioning; in some specific situations, there may be no, or an inverse, correlation. Indeed, the theoretical foundations of bureaucracy are based on *impersonality.* And even with the modern role conception of the modern manager—which includes social system management and responsibility—the prevailing norms of legitimacy of organizational influence must be explored and understood fully by the target system.

- *In undertaking any planned social change, the effects on the adjacent and interdependent subsystems relating to the target system must be carefully considered.*

All three cases demonstrate this principle, but perhaps none so dramatically as in the "Letter from Medical Division." Here we see so clearly how the reverberations and repercussions of laboratory training come back to haunt its creators unless the shock can be absorbed by their neighboring units. In this case, the company doctors could have easily absorbed the shock (as they later did after an orientation session) if they had been simply informed about and involved in laboratory training. They were irked because they were ignored and disturbed by perceived encroachment on their authority. But whether it is doctors or headquarters or colleagues or bosses, a complete diagnosis of the total effects on all relevant parts must be made before, not after, the training starts.

- *In undertaking any planned social change, the state of cultural readiness must be assessed.*

We emphasized this in the preceding section in terms of the internal state of the target system. Here we mean more. We have in mind the relationship between the organization and the wider society within which the target system is embedded. It would appear that Mr. Jones (and Dr. A, to some extent) failed to comprehend completely the normative structure they were attempting to alter. The values of President Hess were known well in advance of the training failure, and he reflected the German cultural values of the farming communities his stores prospered in. Cultural readiness is linked to the normative structure of the wider society; a clear diagnosis cannot be made without understanding these forces.

A POSTSCRIPT ON THE PROSPECTS FOR DEMOCRATIC SOCIAL CHANGE

The preceding eight principles provide only a partial view of the complex elements that enter into organization development. This complexity, along with the drama of the failures, probably tends to make it seem more hazardous than it need be. If we have tended to highlight the dilemmas and risks we do this with the hope that the recognition of these choice points by the people who install and maintain similar organization development programs will enhance their effectiveness.

Ultimately, we believe, the forces for change in the direction of laboratory training's stated goals will gather more and more momentum in our society. There is some evidence for this belief already. But there are other environmental forces at work as well which portend even further acceleration of democratic processes (Bennis and Slater, 1968). There is a rapid rate of technological change, and there is a rapid infusion of professionals into organizations. These circumstances represent two of the most important factors in the outlook for change. And laboratory training, with its particular set of change goals, may provide an important instrument for building organizations where effective collaboration and adaptation can take place.

6

RECONSIDERATIONS

Out of all this has come the first clear recognition of an inescapable fact: we cannot successfully *force* people to work for management's objectives. The ancient conception that people will do the work of the world only if they are forced to do so by threats or intimidation, or by the camouflaged authoritarian methods of paternalism, has been suffering from a lingering fatal illness for a quarter of a century. I venture the guess that it will be dead in another decade.

Douglas McGregor, 1950

McGregor may have been overly optimistic about the death of authoritarianism, but he was unerring, as usual, in putting his finger on the right issue. Given the retroactive insight of almost 20 years, we can say that organization development is essentially an evolutionary process. It asserts that every age develops an organizational form and life style most appropriate to the genius of that age. Most organizations reflect the uneasiness of transition for they were built upon certain assumptions about man and his environment. The environment was thought to be placid, predictable, and uncomplicated. Man was thought to be placid, predictable, and uncomplicated. Organizations based on these assumptions will fail, if not today, then tomorrow. They will fail for the very same reasons that dinosaurs failed: the environment changes suddenly at the peak of their success.[1]

The environment now is busy, clogged, and dense with opportunities and threats; it is turbulent, uncertain, and dynamic. The people who work for organizations are more complicated than ever before. They have needs, motives, anxieties, and to make matters even more complicated, they bring higher expectations than ever before to our institutions. The institutions themselves are changing, through the press of environmental challenges and the internal demands of its people. Organization development is a response to these complex challenges, an educational strategy which aims to bring about a better fit between the human beings who work in and expect things from organizations and the busy, unrelenting environment with its insistence on adapting to changing times.

This is a tremendous task. One should not expect sudden success from such a new practice, I suppose, but it might be useful to examine in this final chapter some of the unsolved problems facing organization development. In doing so, the hope exists that organization development's potential can be realized, rather than forfeiting future achievement through a complacency about current accomplishments. In my view, organization development will be unable to reach its true strength unless it confronts a series of practical, tough problems. The remainder of this chapter will deal briefly with these.

THE POLITICS OF CHANGE

Organization development practitioners rely exclusively on two sources of influence: truth and love. Somehow the hope prevails that man is reasonable and caring, and that valid data, coupled with an environment of trust (and love) will bring about the desired change. "All's fair in love and war." It really is, but you really must know which you're playing. Organization development seems most appropriate under conditions of trust, truth,

1 A recent editorial in the *Boston Globe* quoted Benson Snyder, M.I.T. psychiatrist, apropos dinosaurs and change. Musing about a recent trip to some California universities, he wrote: "There is another consequence of this response to rapid change. The climate of society becomes suffused and distrait, positions ossified, and one hears expressions of helplessness increase, like dinosaurs on the plains of mud. Each in his own way frantically puts on more weight and thinks this form of strength will serve him. He doesn't know he has lost touch until the mud reaches the level of his eyes. . . ."

love, and collaboration. But what about conditions of war, conflict, dissent, and violence? Putting it differently, there seems to be a fundamental deficiency in models of change associated with organization development. It systematically avoids the problem of power, or the *politics* of change.

This deficiency is serious enough from a theoretical point of view, but it is more deadly in practice. For, fundamentally, the organization development consultant tends to use the truth-love model when it may be inappropriate and has no alternative model to guide his practice under conditions of distrust, violence, and conflict. Essentially, this means that in pluralistic power situations, in situations which are not easily controlled, organization development practice may not reach its desired goals. This may explain why organization development has been reasonably successful in industry and other closed, hierarchical structures where power is relatively centralized and there is a basic (if uneven) consensus about organizational goals. At the same time, organization development, to my knowledge, has not met with success in diffuse power structures such as cities, large-scale national organizations, or the urban ghetto.

Another concern that stems from this almost total reliance on the truth-love strategy of social change is that only the wealthy organizations and those with firm control over their constituents can be reached through present organization development programs, leading to what Blake and Mouton refer to as "corporate Darwinism," or more simply, the rich get richer. So IBM, Esso, Union Carbide, ALCAN, AT&T, etc., reap more advantages, while impoverished and disadvantaged groups, such as local government, civil rights movements, universities, hospitals, and communities, are untended.

Still another equally serious problem has to do with the T-group coloration that almost all organization development programs take on. I said in Chapter 1 that organization development should not be confused with sensitivity training or T-groups, but the very fact that I *had* to say it indicates the confusion people have about organization development. Most organization development cases that finally reach print focus almost exclusively on the T-group as the basic strategy of intervention. In the *Journal of Behavioral Sciences,* I wrote an editorial recently which underlined this point (1968, p. 228).

I have yet to see an organization development program that uses an interventional strategy other than an interpersonal one, and this is serious when one considers that the most pivotal strategies of change in our society are political, legal, and technological. We call ourselves change agents,' but the real changes in our society have been wrought by the pill, the bomb, the automobile, industrialization, communication media, and other forces of modernization. The change agents in our society are the lawyers, the architects, the engineers, the politicians, and the assassins. (I should add students to this list, for even as I write this they are rioting and shooting and clamoring for 'real power,' institutional leverage which they have never before sought.)''

I have no easy answer to this dilemma that faces every organization development consultant and change agent: How can he operate in situations of dissension and conflict to help people in those situations to discover and affirm the values of collaboration and commit themselves to its achievement?

Recently (Bennis, Benne, and Chin, 1969, p. 153) I set forth some general principles that may lead toward a wiser handling of the dilemma:

1. Collaboration is an achievement, not a given condition. The ways of effective collaboration must be learned.

2. Conflict is not to be avoided by a change agent. Rather, he faces conflict in himself and in others and seeks ways to channel the aggressive energies of conflict and power toward the achievement of personal and social gain for all concerned.

3. Power is not a bad thing, though much behavioral-science literature treats it as such through indifference or ignorance.

4. Social action depends on power just as physical movement depends on energy. Nothing changes in human affairs until new power is generated or until old power is redistributed.

5. The organization development consultant strives to utilize power that is based on and guided by rationality, valid knowledge, and collaboration and to discount power based on and channeled by fear, irrationality, and coercion. The latter kind of power leads to augmented resistance to change, unstable changes, and dehumanized and irrational conflicts. Still and all, one had better understand these irrational and powerful forces.

Unless models can be developed that include the dimensions of power conflict in addition to truth-love, organization development will find fewer and narrower institutional avenues open to its influence. And in so doing, it will slowly and successfully decay.

STRUCTURE VERSUS CLIMATE

Organization development pays lip service only to structural (or technological) changes while relying only on a change in organizational "climate." I mean by "climate" a set of values or attitudes which affect the way people relate to each other, such as "openness," authority patterns, social relations, etc. This is no mean feat, of course, but again—related to the preceding point—it is seriously restrictive. The organization development literature is filled with vague promises about "restructuring" or "organizational design" but with some exceptions (e.g., Argyris, 1964; Likert, 1967) few outcomes are actually demonstrated. Program budgeting, computerization, new communication systems, structural imagination, "open posting" of new positions (e.g., Polaroid plan), a job enlargement, for example, may have far more impact than a dramatic shift of "organizational climate." It is difficult to understand the effects of climate, as a matter of fact, unless the attitudinal-value complex is reflected in concrete organizational designs. Far more has to be done in bridging an engineering design approach with organization development change strategies before the goal of "socio-technical" approaches can be anything more than respectable jargon.

THE PROFESSION OF ORGANIZATION DEVELOPMENT

Typically, a "profession" is considered to be a "calling" based on a foundation of knowledge directed toward a "clientèle" and with an ethical posture toward its clientèle and members of the profession. To some extent, the practice of organization development is a profession with a growing number of competent practitioners. In other ways, it falls short when compared with other more mature professional callings.

Several areas of concern come to mind. For one thing, there is no integrated theory of organizational change with a set of interrelated hypotheses and variables. This goal is not met, incidentally, in many other professions, such as medicine, law, and engineering. However, and far more serious in my view, is that there is, as yet, no tradition of *adding knowledge cumulatively* to the general theory of practice. The law is established case by case, and in engineering, medicine, and even teaching, there is a steady accumulation upon an accepted framework for practice. I am not aware that organization development is at this stage of development.

Related to this point is the overall disinterest in long-term research projects. Again, with some striking exceptions, the organization development consultant rarely does research on his client system, except for infrequent "evaluation" studies. Now these evaluative studies are terribly important and I do not, in any way, mean to disparage them. But it seems to me that the most significant research to be done on organization development must be related to what organization development is all about, the *development* of an organization over time. Thus, organization development research should deal with long-term processes, induced by certain interventions and leading to certain predictable outcomes. We know a good deal about the interventions—e.g., a confrontation meeting, data feedback, sensitivity training, etc.—and have a moderately good idea of what these interventions do by way of outcomes. We have very little to say about the processes and mechanisms of organizational change. This seems especially paradoxical when the processes of change are exactly what the organization development consultant has to concern himself with.

Most professionals also have on hand a set of instruments which rather quickly assess the client's present health or illness. Organization development practice certainly has a need for a variety of thermometers that can be inserted into the client system in order to identify the status of the client along a whole host of dimensions. For example, an organization development consultant would surely want to examine the value system of the client and the extent to which there was consensus or dissension regarding the core values. An organization development consultant would surely want to understand the nature of the goal structure, communication patterns, decision structure, authority relations, and so on. Over the years, researchers, using a variety of methods from survey methods to group discussion, have been able to develop instrumentation for diagnosis. Yet there is no agreed upon set of instruments to "work up" the diagnosis. This also is paradoxical because organization development practitioners have likely acquired more knowledge about the diagnosis of an organizational system than organizational theorists could tell them.

Much more needs to be said about the training of competent organization development practitioners. The first generation of any new profession is always the most gifted and the most erratic. This is certainly true of organization development practitioners from my vantage point. Some extremely gifted practitioners like Richard Beckhard, Herb Shepard, and Shel Davis, are making history through their creative practice. Others, I am afraid, can possibly jeopardize the growth of organization development in the usual ways that new professions become vulnerable: through routine hackwork, malpractice, and ethical blunders. My main concern here is that we educate and then develop the next generation of organization development practitioners. The universities are not doing it; in fact, my impression is that organizations have "rolled their own," that is, set up their own training programs, independent of the university. There is a lot to be said for that, of course, but homemade programs require nourishment from other sources of knowledge and theory not necessarily contained within organizations. In a sense, I am challenging universities to open their doors to new departments of organization development, applied social sciences, policy sciences, etc. The name is not important. What is important is the need for well-trained full-time practitioners of organization development. For without these new men, who will design the future and help create the organizations that can release our human potential and master the environment?

Expressing these qualms, I hope, will not discourage the reader. Rather, I hope to inspire him, for basically, organization development is one of the few educational programs I know of that has the potential to create an institution vital enough to cope with the unparalleled changes ahead.

REFERENCES AND SELECTED BIBLIOGRAPHY

An Action Research Program for Organization Improvement (in Esso Standard Oil Co.) (1960), Ann Arbor, Michigan, Foundation for Research on Human Behavior.

Argyris, C. (1964), *Integrating the Individual and the Organization,* New York, Wiley.

Argyris, C. (1962), *Interpersonal Competence and Organizational Effectiveness,* Homewood, Ill., Irwin-Dorsey.

Argyris, C. (1967), *Some Causes of Organizational Ineffectiveness within the Department of State,* Washington, D. C., Department of State.

Argyris, C. (1964), "T-groups for organizational effectiveness," *Harvard Business Review,* March-April, pp. 60-74.

Argyris, C. (1960), *Understanding Organizational Behavior,* Homewood, Ill., Dorsey Press.

Bass, B. M. (1965), *Organizational Psychology,* Boston, Allyn and Bacon.

Baumgartel, H. (1959), "Using employee questionnaire results for improving organizations," *Kansas Business Review,* No. 12, pp. 2-6.

Baumgartel, H., Bennis, W. G., and De, N. (1967), *Readings in Group Development,* Calcutta, India, Asia Press.

Beckhard, R. (1967), "The confrontation meeting," *Harvard Business Review,* Vol. XLV, No. 2, pp. 149-153.

Beerbohm, M. (1966), *Zuleika Dobson,* London, Folio Society.

Bennis, W. G. (1963), "A new role for the behavioral sciences: Effecting organizational change," *Administrative Science Quarterly,* Vol. 8, pp. 125-165.

Bennis, W. G. (1966), *Changing Organizations,* New York, McGraw-Hill.

Bennis, W. G. (1968), "Editorial," *Journal of Applied Behavioral Science,* Vol. 4, No. 2, pp. 227-231.

Bennis, W. G., Benne, K. D., and Chin, R. (1969), *The Planning of Change,* New York, Holt, Rinehart and Winston.

Bennis, W. G., and Peter, Hollis W. (1967), "Applying Behavioral Science for Organizational Change" in *Comparative Theories of Social Change,* Ann Arbor, Michigan, Foundation for Research on Human Behavior.

Bennis, W. G., Schein, E. H., Berlew, D. E., and Steele, F. I. (Eds.) (1968, Rev. Ed.), *Interpersonal Dynamics,* Homewood, Ill., Dorsey Press.

Bennis, W. G., and Slater, P. E. (1968), *The Temporary Society,* New York, Harper and Row.

Blake, R. R., Avis, W. E., and Mouton, J. S. (1967), *Corporate Darwinism,* Houston, Gulf Publishing Co.

Blake, R. R., and Mouton, J. S. (1964), *The Managerial Grid,* Houston, Gulf Publishing Co.

Blake, R. R., Mouton, J. S., Barnes, L. B., and Greiner, L. E. (1964), "Breakthrough in Organization Development," *Harvard Business Review,* Nov.-Dec., pp. 133-155.

Blake, R. R., Shepard, H. A., and Mouton, J. S. (1964), *Managing Intergroup Conflict in Industry,* Houston, Gulf Publishing Co.

Blansfield, M. G. (1962), "Depth analysis of organizational life," *Calif. Management Review,* Winter, pp. 29-42.

Blau, P. M., and Scott, W. R. (1961), *Formal Organizations,* San Francisco, Chandler Publishing Co.

Bradford, L. P., Gibb, J. R., and Benne, K. D. (Eds.) (1964), *T-Group Theory and Laboratory Method: Innovation in Re-education,* New York, Wiley.

Burns, T., and Stalker, G. (1961), *The Management of Innovation*, Chicago, Quadrangle Books.

Clark, C. (1965), "Oxford reformed," *Encounter*, Jan., p. 48.

Cooper, W. W., Leavitt, H. J., and Shelly, M. W. (Eds.) (1964), *New Perspectives in Organization Research*, New York, Wiley.

Drucker, P. (1954), *The Practice of Management*, New York, Harper and Row.

Erikson, E. (1965), *Ontogeny of Ritualization*, paper presented to the Royal Society, June.

Etzioni, A. (1964), *Modern Organizations*, Englewood Cliffs, N. J., Prentice-Hall.

Galbraith, J. K. (1967), *The New Industrial State*, Boston, Houghton-Mifflin.

Gardner, J. W. (1965), *Self Renewal*, New York, Harper and Row.

Greiner, L. E. (1967), "Patterns of organization change," *Harvard Business Review*, May-June, Vol. 45, No. 3.

Guest, R. (1962), *Organizational Change*, Homewood, Ill., Irwin-Dorsey.

Jaques, E. (1951), *The Changing Culture of a Factory*, London, Tavistock Publications.

Kahn, R. L., and Boulding, E. (Eds.) (1964), *Power and Conflict in Organizations*, New York, Basic Books.

Kahn, R. L., Wolfe, D. M., Quinn, R. P., Snoek, J. D., and Rosenthal, R. A., (1964), *Organizational Stress: Studies in Role Conflict and Ambiguities*, New York, Wiley.

Katz, D., and Kahn, R. L. (1967), *The Social Psychology of Organizations*, New York, Wiley.

Kerr, C. (1964), *The Uses of the University*, Cambridge, Mass., Harvard University Press.

Kuriloff, A. H. (1966), *Reality in Management*, New York, McGraw-Hill.

Lawrence, P. R. (1958), *The Changing of Organizational Behavior Patterns*, Cambridge, Mass., Harvard University Press.

Lawrence, P. R., and Lorsch, J. W. (1967), *Organization and Environment—Managing Differentiation and Integration,* Cambridge, Mass., Division of Research, Graduate School of Business Administration, Harvard University.

Leavitt, H. (Ed.) (1963), *Social Science of Organization,* Englewood Cliffs, N.J., Prentice-Hall.

Likert, R. (1967), *The Human Organization, Its Management and Value,* New York, McGraw-Hill.

Likert, R. (1961), *New Patterns of Management,* New York, McGraw-Hill.

Lippitt, R., *et al.* (1961), *The Dynamics of Planned Change,* New York, Holt, Rinehart and Winston.

Litterer, J. (1965), *The Analysis of Organizations,* New York, Wiley.

Litterer, J. (1963), *Organization Structure and Behavior,* New York, Wiley.

Lynton, R. P., and Pareek, U. (1967), *Training for Development,* Homewood, Ill., Irwin.

McGregor, D. (1966), *Leadership and Motivation,* Cambridge, Mass., M.I.T. Press.

McGregor, D. (1960), *The Human Side of Enterprise,* New York, McGraw-Hill.

McGregor, D. (1967), *The Professional Manager,* New York, McGraw-Hill.

Mann, F. C., and Neff, F. W. (1961), *Managing Major Change in Organizations,* Ann Arbor, Michigan, Foundation for Research on Human Behavior.

March, J. G. (Ed.) (1965), *Handbook of Organizations,* Chicago, Rand-McNally.

Marrow, A. J. (1966), "Managerial revolution in the State Department," *Personnel,* Nov.-Dec., pp. 2-12.

Marrow, A. J., Bowers, D. G., Seashore, S. E. (1967), *Management by Participation,* New York, Harper.

Maslow, A. H. (1965), *Eupsychian Management,* Homewood, Ill., Irwin.

Miles, M. B. (1964), *Innovation in Education,* New York, Columbia University, Teachers College Press.

Presthus, R. (1965), *The Organizational Society,* New York, Vintage Books.

Rabbie, J. (1966), verbal communication.

Ready, R. K. (1967), *The Administrator's Job: Issues and Dilemmas,* New York, McGraw-Hill.

Rubenstein, A., and Haberstroh, C. (1966), *Some Theories of Organization* (2nd Ed.), Homewood, Ill., Irwin-Dorsey.

Schein, E. H. (1965), *Organizational Psychology,* Englewood Cliffs, N.J., Prentice-Hall.

Schein, E. H., and Bennis, W. G. (1965), *Personal and Organizational Change Through Group Methods: The Laboratory Approach,* New York, Wiley.

Seiler, J. (1967), *Systems Analysis in Organizational Behavior,* Homewood, Ill., Irwin-Dorsey.

Sofer, C. (1961), *The Organization from Within,* London, Tavistock Publications.

Strauss, G., and Bavelas, A. (1955), "Group Dynamics and Intergroup Relations," in Whyte, W. F., *et al.* (Eds.), *Money and Motivation,* New York, Harper and Row, pp. 90-96.

Tannenbaum, R., *et al.* (1961), *Leadership and Organization,* New York, McGraw-Hill.

Thompson, J. D. (Ed.) (1966), *Approaches to Organizational Design,* Pittsburgh, University of Pittsburgh Press.

Trist, W. L., Higgin, G. W., Murray, H., and Pollock, A. B. (1963), *Organizational Choice,* London, Tavistock Publications.

Vickers, G. (1967), *Toward A Sociology of Management,* New York, Basic Books.

Vroom, H. (1964), *Work and Motivation,* New York, Wiley.

"What is OD?," (1968), *News and Reports,* Vol. 2, No. 3, Washington, D. C., NTL.

What's Wrong with Work?, (1967), New York, National Association of Manufacturers.